Frank J. McGrath

Lord Poverty's Assets

A Comedy in four Acts

Frank J. McGrath

Lord Poverty's Assets
A Comedy in four Acts

ISBN/EAN: 9783337148829

Printed in Europe, USA, Canada, Australia, Japan

Cover: Foto ©ninafisch / pixelio.de

More available books at **www.hansebooks.com**

LORD POVERTY'S ASSETS.

A COMEDY

In Four Acts

BY M. RENARD D'FALCA.

Entered according to Act of Congress, in the year 1896 by Frank J. Mc Grath in the office of the Librarian of Congress, Washington, D. C.

Copyright 1896.
All rights reserved.
Entered at Stationer's Hall.

THE PERSONS OF THE PLAY.

LORD COURTLAND POVERTY.
JONATHAN RUSHFOOT.
OLD MABY.
MR. MABY (his son).
JOHN RANDOLPH ROBINS JR. (Jack).
SIGNIOR SIRAO.
MR. GOWER.
MR. SMILE.
CAPTAIN EMERY.
MAXEY.
TAYLOR.
MRS. SMILE.
MRS. MABY.
HELEN RUSHFOOT (her sister).
EFFIE REVERE.
MISS BENSON.
LADY POVERTY.
SALLY.

MESSENGER, PARADERS, REPORTERS, DETECTIVE, CONSTABLE etc. etc.

LORD POVERTY'S ASSETS.

THE FIRST ACT.

The Scene is the STUDIO of SIGNIOR SIRAO, in an 'appartment on the ground floor of the MABY BUILDING, DORCHESTER OAKS, England. On the spectators left is a door, leading into a small drawing room, that communicates, it is supposed, with appartment hall. Over the door hangs a portière, drawn aside. On the right is an arched entrance, opening into same hall, that leads, it is supposed, to the main hall of the building, through outer doors. On the left is an invisible bay window, commanding a view of the street. On the right is a closed door, that leads, it is supposed, into an empty room. Facing the audience is a large painting in massive gilt frame. The canvas is concealed by rich crimson curtains, drawn, and fastened by locked clasps. Above the painting is a row of gas jets, with reflectors, to illuminate the canvas. On the walls are hung paintings of various sizes. Tables, chairs, large swivelled glass etc. are scattered about the room. A library ladder, used for hanging pictures, stands to the right. No carpet on the floor. The room, though abounding in works of art and rich furniture, suggests temporary occupation only.

TAYLOR, a footman, a pronounced Cockney with loitering air.]

SALLY, a trim young English house-maid, with Cockney accent, dusting and hanging paintings.

TAYLOR.

Hi siy Sally! what's this 'ere [*Pointing to curtained canvas.*] canvas hart picture, that hevery one his talking habout?

SALLY.

Hit's "Peace."

TAYLOR.

Piece of what?

SALLY.

Piece of nothing, Silly! [*Detects* TAYLOR *trying to pull curtains aside to see the painting.*] 'Ey there, Busy! where his your heyes?

TAYLOR.

[*Desists.*] You're so sparing hof your hinformation——

SALLY.

[*Snappishly.*] You've seen pictures hof war, 'aven't you?

TAYLOR.

Aye!

SALLY.

[*Approaching* TAYLOR, *who stands opposite the painting.*] Well this 'ere picture, [*Pointing with handle of duster.*] hisn't habout war, hits peace. [*Proceeding to describe the painting.*] 'Ere, [*Pointing*] his two young lidies awalking, 'and hin 'and;

'ere, his bibies, hand sunny door steps, hand cows; there, his birds haflying; a river, a chapel, a school'ouse—

TAYLOR.

[*Interrupting.*] Hi siy! Miss. [*Laughing.*] These 'ere "peace-cows" hof yours his hin the hair. [*Pointing.*]

SALLY.

[*Properly locating the sky and earth, on painting.*] There his the sky, [*Striking him.*] hand 'ere the hearth. [*Striking him again.*] Now Smarty! see hit?

TAYLOR.

Hi feels hit. [*Putting both hands to his head.*]

SALLY.

Hi 'ad to 'ammer hit hinto your 'ead, Bob. [*Laughing.*]

TAYLOR.

You cut me.

SALLY.

[*Looking at his head.*] Where?

TAYLOR.

[*Affecting to show the cut on his scalp.*] There! [*Kissing her.*]

SALLY.

[*Pouting.*] Give over your nonsense.

TAYLOR.

Aye. [*Approaching* SALLY *who threatens, playfully, to strike him.*] No more Sally. Hi siy, Hi 'eard you were to henter service at Devon 'Ouse, soon.

SALLY.

[*Nodding.*] Aye, parlor mide.

TAYLOR.

R'ember! There's one thing you've got to do hat masters; keep your mouth closed habout what you 'ears habout mines. Remember! hits mum hat masters, haboit mines.

SALLY.

[*Heedless of Taylor's last remark.*] Who was a telling hof you?

TAYLOR.

Hi 'eard hit hat the Tigers.

SALLY.

Hi 'm tired hof this Hitalian, hany way; his abusing of poor Maxey—

TAYLOR.

[*Interrupting.*] Hisn't Maxey some kin of the Dago's?

SALLY.

'Is stepson. 'E killed Maxey's mother.

TAYLOR.

Killed 'er?

SALLY.

Aye, by habusing hof 'er. So Maxey siyes.

TAYLOR.

He 'as no Henglish, you siy?

SALLY.

[*Demonstratively.*] 'E can make signs, cant 'e?

TAYLOR.

You needn't take me 'ead hoff!

SALLY.

Bob, Maxey is a good 'onest lad but e's got han hawful temper. [*Dusting another picture.*]

TAYLOR.

We're hagoing to 'ave ha big time hon the nineteenth, Sally.

SALLY.

At the hopening of the new quarters hof the Harbitration League?
What *his* the Harbitration League Bob?

TAYLOR.

Master siys, hits formed for the purpose of getting Hamerica to hagree, that there wont be no more wars.

SALLY.

No, more wars!

TAYLOR.

Nothing but harbitration.

SALLY.

[*Swings duster.*] 'Urrah! 'urrah! No move Hafrica for John Havery!

TAYLOR.

John Havery. [*With disgust.*] The Hafricans haint going to get no harbitration.

SALLY.

Why not?

TAYLOR.

Hengland honly harbitrates with people, she cant knock habout, Silly.

SALLY.

[*About to hang small painting.*] Fancy! 'Ang this wont you?

TAYLOR.

Aye. [*Ascends ladder.* SALLY *hands him painting.*]

SALLY.

Don't fall.

TAYLOR.

Hit's hat the Jolly Tigers that one hears hevery thing; heven habout you, Sally.

SALLY.

Me?

TAYLOR.

Aye.

SALLY.

[*With an injured air.*] What Bob.

TAYLOR.

Not much. Honly that hof hall the 'ansome lads in Dorchester Hoaks, you most favors me.

SALLY.

[*Throwing duster at* TAYLOR.] The hidea! [*Shakes ladder.*]

TAYLOR.

[*Hanging on and laughing.*] Give hover. Hi'll drop the picture!

SALLY.

[*Shaking.*] The hidea —

TAYLOR.

His hin me hown 'ead. [SALLY *stops.*] This his worse than following the 'ounds hon a tramway nag. [*Hangs picture and comes down.*] No, Sally, the gossip thats hon hevery night at the Tigers, his that Mrs. Miby 'ad 'er husband give this hart picture to the Harbitration League, so 'ed get hinto —

SALLY.

Hinto Parliament. Hevery one knows that.

TAYLOR.

No smarty! She wants 'im knighted. 'E's sure hof parliament, Hi thinks, hif the local hand central clubs hagrees to accept 'im has their candidate for this borough. There's ha big fight hon habout hit. The thing his to be settled to diy.

SALLY.

Hawkins his the hother candidate hisn't 'e Bob?

TAYLOR.

Aye. Some siy, because Mr. Miby was beaten hat the last election, 'e ought n't to run hagain. Hi 'ates these bye election.

SALLY.

Knights hor parliamentarians hit makes no hodds. [*Earnestly.*] Mrs. Miby belongs hup hamong the 'igh folks. [*Moves ladder, and is about to hang another picture*] Give me hanother 'and, Bob. Please.

TAYLOR.

[*Going up the ladder.*] There's no disputing hit Sally; Mrs. Miby his the 'ighest toned lidy hin these 'ere parts, hand some folks hin Dorchester Hoaks his jealous of 'er. [*Confidentially.*] The diy of Lidy Hamilton's reception. Mrs. Smile's coachman got 'is walking ticket because 'e turned hout in the road, too far, to let Mrs. Mibys carriage pass. Mrs. Smile gave hout, that 'e was drinking too much.

SALLY.

Nonsense! Mrs. Smile hand Mrs. Miby his like sisters.

TAYLOR.

Mrs. Smile his ha snake hin the grass. Some diy your mistrees will find hit hout. [*Comes down ladder. Puts his foot through small painting, that's on floor.*]

SALLY.

[*Screams.*] Oh Bob, hits ruined!

TAYLOR.

So ham Hi! What mide you leave hit there for, Stupid?

SALLY.

Hits done for!

TAYLOR.

[*Taking picture off his foot.*] So ham Hi! hand you too, Careless!

SALLY.

What'll we do?

TAYLOR.

'Ere. [*Hands painting to* SALLY.] 'Ide hit, 'ide hit! [*Looking into the hall.*] Mrs. Smile his hacoming, [*Startled:*] 'ide hit. [*Forcing it on* SALLY.]

SALLY.

[*Snappishly.*] I cant swallow hit!

TAYLOR.

Cover hit hup; she won't see hit! [*Puts cord over* SALLY'S *head, the painting hanging down back, face to. Takes her apron and turns it around, partly concealing picture,*]

SALLY.

[*Almost in tears.*] She's 'ere! She's — — [*Enters* MRS. SMILE, *a tall, handsome, well bred woman, about thirty two, good looking, charming manners, and winning smile, quick perception adroit and watchful. Her whole bearing is that of a lady, of delicate temperament; yet when aroused, she descends to the coarseness of profanity. At heart, she is a jealous, re-*

vengeful hypocrite, stopping at nothing to accomplish her purpose.

Mrs. SMILE.

Mr. Smile not here! [*Sees* SALLY, *who stands with her back to the wall near right entrance, clutching portière.*] Alone, Sally? [TAYLOR, *who has taken a position near the left entrance, for the purpose of escaping unobserved, retires.*] Not quite, I see. [*Catching a glimpse of* TAYLOR, *as he goes out.*]

SALLY.

[*Who has not heard* MRS. SMILE'S *last remark.*] Yes, Madame.

MRS. SMILE.

[*To herself.*] The lying creature! [*To* SALLY, *coldly.*] Where is Signior Sirao?

SALLY.

Hat Devon House, Madame.

MRS. SMILE.

[*Surprised. At once assuming an agreeable*

manner. To herself.] What's up? [*To* SALLY.] How neat and well you are looking!

SALLY.

Thank you, madame.

MRS. SMILE.

[*Looking in glass.*] So Signior Sirao has gone to Devon House.

SALLY.

Yes, madame.

MRS. SMILE.

Drops a pin on the floor, while arranging her hair and hat.] Sally, come pick up my pin. [SALLY *hesitates.*] You'll find it near the chair. [*Looking in direction of chair.*] I think it's there. [*Pointing with her foot, looks in glass again* SALLY. *Taking advantage of* Mrs. SMILES *preoccupation hastens to obey.* Mrs. SMILE *looks toward Sally, who is now bending over.*] What on earth have you got on? [*Drops her hands from her head, and laughs.*] Off all the — a painting!

SALLY.

One that's broke. [*Commencing to cry.*]

MRS. SMILE.

[*Examining painting.*] The very one I was going to buy. [TAYLOR, *wo has been loitering in the hall, to see the outcome of* MRS. SMILES *discovery, looks in.*] Whose work is this?

SALLY.

Me and Taylor's — mostly mine. [*Enters* TAYLOR.]

TAYLOR.

Yes marm — mostly Sally's.

MRS. SMILE.

I'm sorry for you. [*To herself.*] I'll turn the gossiping tongue of this footman, to good account. [SALLY *still cries, and* TAYLOR *stands with bowed head. To* TAYLOR.] I will help you out of your trouble, on one condition; that is, that you hold your tongue. No one must know, that I am capable of excusing such negligence.

TAYLOR.

Hi'll never hopen my mouth habout hit, marm.

MRS. SMILE.

[*To* SALLY.] Take the painting to my house immediately! I'll buy it, and sacrifice to your carelessness, the money I had intended for a local charity.

SALLY.

Thank you madame; thank you! [*Attempts to take picture off.*]

MRS. SMILE.

Never mind, go! [*Exit Sally. With affected severity.*] I shall have to sell some of my Extension shares to pay for this painting. You know how valuable they are!

TAYLOR.

Hif you means, marm, the Gold Slopper shares, hevery body knows they comes 'igh.

MRS. SMILE.

I mean the Extension; you know all about it. [*Stamps her foot.*]

TAYLOR.

Hi honly 'eard Mr. Rushfoot siy, 'e was afraid the mine was no good.

MRS. SMILE.

[*To herself.*] This information is valuable. [*To* TAYLOR.] I dont wish to know, what, either Mr. Rushfoot, or Mr. Maby says. Now go!

TAYLOR.

Thank you marm. [*Aside.*] She's got ha lot hout hof me! [*Laughs Exit* TAYLOR.]

MRS. SMILE.

He must sell! My husband must be in the building; I'll find him. [*Exit.*]

[*Enters* SIRAO *and* MAXEY.] SIRAO. [*A small, dark skinned, clean shaven, Italian jew about forty. Nervous, polite and well dressed. Has a habit of drawing his mouth to one side, and inhaling* the air through his closed teeth, making an audible noise; that at times, is disgusting.] Do you hear me Maxey? [*Laughing.*] Yes you hear me, but you dont understand.

MAXEY.

[*A handsome, pale faced Italian boy, about thirteen. Large sorrowful eyes, and dark wavy hair. Though cleanly dressed, his clothes are too small. When greatly angered, his features become transformed. In such paroxysms he is wildly desperate.*[Parlate italiano per piacere. (*Please talk Italian.*) [*Examines reflectors and gas jets.*]

SIRAO.

No, if I talked Italian, you would understand. [*Laughs. Takes up a small painting. looks at it.*] Fix the reflectors good, Maxey. Light is ninety percent of the business. [*Laughs.*] I bought "Rebecca at The Well", by Garriden, for seven hundred pounds. [*Laughs.*] The light was poor? the janitor was a friend of mine. The Countess of Flanders gave me three thousand pounds for it; she saw it under an inspiring glare. [*Laughs, and shows his teeth.*] You see, Maxey, when I do business, I do it open, and in the light. [*Examines small painting.*] My gracious! what is this?

MAXEY.

"L'uomo onesto" di Smith. (*Smith's Honest Man.*)

SIRAO.

"Smith's Honest Man"! Yes, but this is the the original. I told you to put the copy in the frame. [*Shakes him.*] You—d—d, you, damn Maxey! [*Strikes, and shakes him again.*] When I tell you to frame copies, I mean copies! [MAXEY *struggles to get away*.

MAXEX.

Lasciate mi andare. (*Let me go!*)

SIRAO.

[*Thinking someone is entering, desists.*] It was only a mistake of judgment, Maxey; [*Pleasantly.*] an honest business mistake. [*Goes to left entrance. Discovers no one entering.*] Let you go, you show fight to your father, do you!

MAXEY.

[*Gesticulating wildly.*] Voi non siete mio padre. (You are not my father.)

SIRAO.

Not your father? you damn Maxey! [*Trys to catch him.*]

MAXEY.

[*Running to escape him.*] Andate via, andate via. (*Go way, go way.*)

SIRAO.

Tell me to go way, you devil! [MAXEY *backs out toward entrance, and disappears.*] Damn Maxey! he's like his mother. [*Unlocks clasps, and draws curtains aside.*] When I leave Dorchester Oaks, I'll let him go. Yes, to the devil; and I will leave soon; before the Celebration. [*Laughs. Turns on lights. Scrutinizes painting.*] All right, all right! [*Exit* SIRAO. *Enter* LORD POVERTY *and* LADY POVERTY, *his mother.*]

LADY POVERTY.

[*An aristocratic looking elderly lady. Gray hair, and dressed in mourning.*] Courtland, remember your mother is a woman.

LORD POVERTY.

[*An augular Englishman, about twenty eight. Fashionably and scrupulously attired with high collar and four—in—hand tie.— Is cleanly shaven, has dark, strait hair, brushed close to his head, and parted in the middle. Pronounced features, with absolute immobility of expression. Precipitous in speech, with jerky, strong, ascending intonation from the first word of a sentence, to nearly its close. When though his tone becomes less pronounced it still rises to a close that's always abrupt. While apparently cold, he's possessed of a warm heart and beneath, what appears to be an almost stupid mind, is quick perception, and good sense.*] A woman — of course. [*Looking at painting.*] Very fine.

LADY POVERTY.

[*Absorbed in the conversation with her son.*] Helen Rushfoot is eligible.

LORD POVERTY.

Fancy.

LADY POVERTY.

Lady Hamilton has so decided. [*Looks at painting.*]

LORD POVERTY.

Decided — of course; but suppose the girl wont have me?

LADY POVERTY.

Nonsense!

LORD POVERTY.

Very well, I'll scheme away at her.

LADY POVERTY.

Yes, delicately and earnestly.

LORD POVERTY.

Delicately — to be sure. Why not?

LADY POVERTY.

Remember, it takes four thousand a year to keep up your aunt's estate. She leaves you one half of that sum, provided you marry an equal amount. Failing in this, the Baron becomes her heir.

LORD POVERTY.

Her heir — to be sure. To inherit money, I must marry cash.

LADY POVERTY.

That's it.

LORD POVERTY.

No wedding cash — no funeral stuff.

LADY POVERTY.

Lady Hamilton has so decreed it.

LORD POVERTY.

Suppose Lady Hamilton should die, in the midst of me campaign?

LADY POVERTY.

Trust to events. She'll reward your good intentions, no doubt; 'and rest assured, she'll be advised of your efforts.

LORD POVERTY.

Advised — of course, by that old cat of hers.

LADY POVERTY.

[*Earnestly.*] Yes, look out for Benson. [*Looking toward left entrance.*] And here she comes! [*Enters* MISS BENSON, *an old, dried up spinster.*]

BENSON.

Your ladyship. [*Courtesying, old style.*] Your lordship. [*Courtesying, again. Hands* LADY POVERTY *a letter.*]

LADY POVERTY.

[*Looking at Letter.*] From the Baron; your aunt wants me to read it. [*Looks toward left entrance; sees* HELEN RUSHFOOT *coming. To* LORD POVERTY.] Miss Rushfoot is in the hall and she's alone. [*To* BENSON.] Come into the drawing room. [BENSON *courtesys to* LADY POVERTY.] I'll read the letter there. [*To* LORD POVERTY.] Remember, earnestly and delicately.

LORD POVERTY.

Why not? [*Exeunt* LADY POVERTY *and* BENSON. *The latter manages to catch a glimpse of* HELEN, *as she enters, by purposely tarrying to make a courtesy to* LORD POVERTY.]

LORD POVERTY.

[*Looking at* BENSON.] She's not fat. [*To* HELEN *as she approaches.*] I'm glad to see you— of course.

HELEN.

[*A pretty bright young lady of eighteen.*] Lord Poverty, and alone?

LORD POVERTY.

No, me mother and me aunt's cat are in the drawing room. [LADY POVERTY, *hearing her son's last remark, coughs loudly to drown his words, as well as to warn him, against further indiscretions of speech.*]

HELEN.

[*Laughing.*] Your aunt's cat?

LORD POVERTY.

Yes — Benson. [LADY POVERTY, *who can be seen in the drawing room, near the entrance, nervously rubs her hands, and coughs again.*]

HELEN.

Oh! [*Laughs.*] Where did you leave father? [*Looks at painting.*] Beautiful! Its grandeur seems to increase, day by day.

LORD POVERTY.

Your father — he left me — to buy the states.

HELEN.

The states?

LORD POVERTY.

Yes — your own states, of course. They've made a new map about them.

HELEN.

Oh yes! a map of the United States.

LORD POVERTY.

That's it!

HELEN.

[*Confidentially.*] Father is going home after the nineteenth. You ought to go with him.

LORD POVERTY.

Why not?

HELEN.

You didn't see much of the United States, when you were there last; yet you've been nearly nine years in India.

LORD POVERTY.

Of course — I saw only Colorado.

HELEN.

Father would be delighted to have you go.

LORD POVERTY.

But you see, I'm waiting.

HELEN.

Waiting?

LORD POVERTY.

Yes — for a little luck; a bit of grave yard luck; [*Coughing in the drawing room.*]

HELEN.

Grave yard luck?

LORD POVERTY.

Of course — you see I've an old aunt, who's bothering along with a bit of breath in her. [LADY POVERTY *disappears from view, coughing, and immediately after a piano is heard playing, an old tune, in a doleful, and jerky manner. This continues during,* LORD POVERTY'S *dialogue with* HELEN. *The music varies from high to low thumping notes, as* LORD POVERTY'S *indiscretions of speech justify.*] when that leaves her, I'm to have two thousand a year.

HELEN.

[*Holding her breath, with comical expression of horror, at* LORD POVERTY'S *cold blooded remarks.*] Lord Poverty!

LORD POVERTY.

[*Without noticing* HELEN'S *last remark.*] And then I don't mind doing the States.

HELEN.

[*With affected indignation mingled with uncontrollable mirth.*] Lady Hamilton ought not to leave you a dollar.

LORD POVERTY.

Of course — the cemetery ticket may prove a blank. If it does, I'll jog along to the States — why not?

HELEN.

[*Sarcastically.*] In search. no doubt, of some American girl with money.

LORD POVERTY.

With money — of course. I'd knock about a little for the money — to be sure.

HELEN.

The money! What about the girl?

LORD POVERTY.

The girl — yes, yes — of course — the poor thing — I forgot about her, but the inheritance trick suits me best.

HELEN.

Lord Poverty, I'm surprised!

LORD POVERTY.

Ah — but it's better. The legacy trick is always the best. In that case, you see, the money's yours; but when a girl bribes a chap to marry her, she's forever after picking away at his subsidy, begging a pound for this thing, and a shilling for that.

HELEN.

[*Solemnly and searchingly.*] Then the girl you marry, must have money.

LORD POVERTY.

Of course — I'm forbidden to bother with anything but cash.

HELEN.

And to please Lady Hamilton —

LORD POVERTY.

Not to please her — to get her money.

HELEN.

Lord Poverty, you can never be a friend of mine; [*Sorrowfully and looking downward.*] and I wanted you to be so much.

LORD POVERTY.

So much — of course.

HELEN.

I wanted some one to confide in —

LORD POVERTY.

I'll take your confidence.

HELEN.

For I'm friendless, and in a foreign land.

LORD POVERTY.

I'll be your friend — why not?

HELEN.

[*Looking at* LORD POVERTY *inquiringly*.] Will you?

[*Collecting herself.*] No, no, your too cold, too cold to understand the sorrows of a young girls baffled affections.

LORD POVERTY.

Are you in love?

HELEN.

[*Nods assent.*] Yes — but you don't know, what it is, to be that way. [*Nervously working her foot and looking at her shoe.*]

LORD POVERTY.

Who's the chap?

HELEN.

Would you like to meet him?

LORD POVERTY.

Why not?

HELEN.

[*Looking toward ceiling.*] But he's away-way off accross the wide, wide — [*Looking at* LORD POVERTY.] Will you never tell?

LORD POVERTY.

[*Shakes his head.*] Never.

HELEN.

While you live, and I live and Jack lives?

LORD POVERTY.

While anybody lives.

HELEN.

He's away off across the wide, wide — street.

LORD POVERTY.

At the hotel?

HELEN.

Yes, just arrived from America. He's registered as Jack Randolph, but his real name is John, Randolph Robins Jr. Father exiled me [*Sorrowfully.*] to prevent me from seeing Jack, and all because he heard, that Jack was wild, but he isn't. [*Putting handkerchief to her eyes.*] Father has condemned him, without a trial, without even, ever having seen him.

LORD POVERTY.

I'm afraid, I cant help you. I can't help myself.

HELEN.

[*Turning her head, but with handkerchief still to her eyes.*] Why?

LORD POVERTY.

I'm in the same boat as yourself.

HELEN.

Are you in love?

LORD POVERTY.

Why not?

HELEN.

[*With delight.*] Oh! Isn't that nice! [*Reflecing.*] But I understand, she's got money.

LORD POVERTY.

No— she's a poor thing.

HELEN.

And you love her, in spite of Lady Hamilton's wishes.

LORD POVERTY.

I'm to trick me aunt.

HELEN.

[*Excitedly*]. Do you want help?

LORD POVERTY.

Of course.

HELEN.

I'll help you, if you'll help me.

LORD POVERTY.

Who are you going to trick.

HELEN.

Nobody — I only want you to help me see Jack, every day. What's your girls name?

LORD POVERTY.

Will you never tell?

HELEN.

Never!

LORD POVERTY.

Until you're dead — I mean — while nobody lives?

HELEN.

[*Laughing.*] I'll never tell.

LORD POVERTY.

Effie Lillian Maloney Revere.

HELEN.

[*Surprised.*] Not the chapel organist?

LORD POVERTY.

Who else?

HELEN.

Why she's an American.

LORD POVERTY.

From Colorado.

HELEN.

Oh, Lord Poverty! — she's the most beautiful girl in Dorchester Oaks. Does she love you?

LORD POVERTY.

She's too busy.

HELEN.

And you love her?

LORD POVERTY.

Why not?

HELEN.

Can't you find out, whether or not she loves you?

LORD POVERTY.

I'm working away at her.

HELEN.

That's the way Jack did to me.

LORD POVERTY.

I'll see Jack, [*Reflects.*] and get him to be an newspaper chap— [*Reflects again.*] an art critic. That'll keep him knocking about you until the nineteenth.

HELEN.

That's splendid! [*With impatience.*] see him right away.

LORD POVERTY.

[*Taking his stick and hat from table.*] Here's the way you can help me.

HELEN.

How?

LORD POVERTY.

Be mushed on me. [HELEN *laughs.*] Isn't that what the Americans call it?

HELEN.

[*Still laughing,*] No — mashed!

LORD POVERTY.

Mashed — of course. Pretend to be mashed on me, whenever Benson is about. You see, Lady Hamilton wants me to give up Maloney.

HELEN.

[*Laughs.*] Maloney! [*Anxious to have him go.*] Yes, yes, but tell Jack tell him that I'm going to pretend to love you. [*Gesticulating.*] I don't want to— [*Laughing.*] I couldn't! Remember, Jack's awfully jealous.

LORD POVERTY.

Of course. [*Goes toward left entrance.*]

HELEN.

[*Excited.*] See him at once — make him an art critic! I must find father.

LORD POVERTY.

I'll see you to your carriage. [*Exeunt* LORD POVERTY *and* HELEN. *Music in drawing room ceases. Enter* LADY POVERTY *and* BENSON.]

LADY POVERTY.

I'm so fond of music. [*To herself.*] What a son! [*To* BENSON.] I'm so fond of music. [*To herself.*] Oh! my poor rheumatic fingers; they're nearly broken. [*To* BENSON.] The charms of music! [*Exit, trying to straighten her fingers, followed by* BENSON. *Enter* MR. *and* MRS. SMILE. *bowing to* LADY POVERTY, *who has passed them, in the hall.*]

MR. SMILE.

[*A fashionably dressed, middle aged, voluptuous looking man. Wears a monocle, has light hair, curled mustache. Affects the English swell.*] By Jove! Poverty is on the track of money at last.

MRS. SMILE.

That man is an enigma to me. [*Looks into drawing room to see if any one is there.*] No one!

MR. SMILE.

No riddle to me.

MRS. SMILE.

Then explain his attentions to the organist?

MR. SMILE.

He's given her up.

MRS. SMILE.

[*Scornfully.*] Mrs. Maby wouldn't object to Lord Poverty as a brother-in-law. Eh? I'm getting so I despise the Rushfoots, and the Mabys too! Old Rushfoot ex-cattle king, cowboy, miner and millionaire.

MR. SMILE.

Lizzie, you're a good hater. Ha, ha, ha — You thought more of Emma than you did of me, when you were at school together.

MRS. SMILE.

[*Excitedly.*] See how she repays me!

MR. SMILE.

Now dear, don't!

MRS. SMILE.

She permited the husband of her dearest friend, to be precipitated into the vortex of bankruptcy, when by a nod she could have saved him. [*With emotion.*] My tears moved her not. [*Collecting herself.*] She had a motive.

MR. SMILE.

A motive?

MRS. SMILE.

Yes — the social life of Dorchester Oaks was too circumscribed, for her to share it's first honors, with even her dearest friend. [*Laughing.*] How I do rave, when I think!

MR. SMILE.

That's right, forget it!

MRS. SMILE.

Forget it! You dont know your own wife!

MR. SMILE.

[*To divert her thoughts.*] By the way, who in the devil is this Yankee organist?

MRS. SMILE.

Nobody knows except the Dominie; and who ever heard of his telling anything?

MR. SMILE.

He adopted her, did he not?

MRS. SMILE.

[*Looking at hanging pictures.*] Yes, when she was eleven years old.

MR. SMILE.

I heard, that he found her, somewhere in Colorado.

MRS. SMILE.

Probably, he was in America nine years ago.

MR. SMILE.

By Jove! she's a stunning looking girl. The Dominie is poor, isn't he?

MRS. SMILE.

Very.

MR. SMILE.

How in the devil can he afford to dress her so?

MRS. SMILE.

Thats one of the mysteries of Dorchester Oaks.

MR. SMILE.

They tell me at the club, that the Dominie hardly knows her.

MRS. SMILE.

She's been away at school all the time.

MR. SMILE.

It's an odd fact, that when the Dominie adopted her, he did not insist on having her, change her name.

MRS. SMILE.

Oh, dear! — all these facts have been discussed, time and time again, in every household in Dorchester Oaks. What do you suppose Mrs. Maby wanted of Signior Sirao?

MR. SMILE.

I know. [*Looks at his wife, as though doubting the wisdom of telling her.*] Now Lizzie, keep cool.

MRS. SMILE.

[*Aroused.*] Out with it!

MR. SMILE.

His Royal Highness, the Prince of Wales, is to be present at the opening of the headquarters, of the Arbitration League; and — [*Hesitates.*]

MRS. SMILE.

Go on!

MR. SMILE.

His Highness, with three members of the Royal household, is to remain over night at Devon House.

MRS. SMILE.

[*Greatly agitated by conflicting emotions.*] Damn the Prince of Wales! [*In tragic tones.*]

MR. SMILE.

[*Alarmed.*] Hush!

MRS. SMILE.

This means, "My Lady Maby". [*Laughing long and loud — noise in hall.*] What's that? [*Enters* MAXEY, *backing in from left entrance adjusting his clothes and shaking his head.*]

MAXEY.

Me killa him! [SALLY *appears, dressed to go out, with small painting wrapped in a paper under her arm.*]

SALLY

Come with me, Maxey. [*Trys to convey her meaning to him by gestures.*]

MAXEY.

[*Seeing* MRS. SMILE.] Lada, Lada! [*Pointing to picture, under* SALLY'S *arm.*] No gooda, no gooda! [*Snatches painting from* SALLY, *and tears wrapping off.*] No gooda! Egli e' furbo an noms casttins — [*He's a cheat, a bad cheat!*] Sirao cheata —

MRS. SMILE.

The boy is mad!

MR. SMILE.

Let him alone!

MAXEY.

Lada, not origa! [*Tears the canvas out of frame, and stamps on it.*]

MRS. SMILE.

What does he mean?

MR. SMILE.

He says its not the original. He knows what he's doing.

MAXEY.

[*Beckons* to MRS. SMILE. *Takes a knife out of his pocket, and going to door on the left, opens it by prying the bolt back with knife.*]

MRS. SMILE.

What is he after?

MR. SMILE.

I have no idea.

MRS. SMILE.

[*Looking into the empty room.*] An empty room!

MR. SMILE.

Empty! its filled with unframed paintings.

MRS. SMILE.

[*Surprised.*] There's "Van Elfins Peace!"

MR. SMILE.

Yes, so it is! and a fine copy too. By Jove, its grand!

MAXEY.

[*Taking painting from room, closes the door, and locks it again. To* MRS. SMILE.] Lada, origa! [*Pointing to the painting he takes from room.*] Origa, origa. — [*Gives it to* SALLY. *Exit* MAXEY. SALLY *retires.*]

MRS. SMILE.

[*Looking at her husband.*] What does all this mean! [*Reflects. Looks at great painting.*] Get Maxey! Quick! Hurry!

MR. SMILE.

By Jove! you should have kept him! [*Exit* SMILE *hastily.*]

MRS. SMILE.

[*Looking again at painting.*] Can it be possible! [*Laughs.*] I must see the boy! [*Exit. Enters* MR. MABY *and* GORDON GOWER.]

GOWER.

[*A large, dull, conceited looking man, about sixty.*] The committees decide to day do they.

MR. MABY.

[*A quiet unassuming man, about thirty five. Good looking and well dressed.*] Yes, I think they 'll want me to stand.

MR. GOWER.

They may. By the way, I have never met your father-in-law.

MR. MABY.

I expect him here, every minute.

GOWER.

I want to ask him about the Extension.

MR. MABY.

Are you a shareholder? [*Enter* MR. *and* MRS. SMILE. *Both bow to* MABY *and* GOWER, *who bow in return.*]

MR. SMILE.

I couldn't see across the street — it's dark [MRS. SMILE, *shows signs of inpatience.*]

GOWER.

Yes, I took some shares for a debt. [*Noise in the street. Enters* HELEN.]

HELEN.

What can all this noise mean?

MR. MABY.

[*Goes to the window.*] An unusual commotion in the street. Here comes Lord Poverty; he may know the cause of the excitement. [*Enter* LORD POVERTY *and* JACK. HELEN *on right, looks at Jack with admiration, yet solicitous, as to how he will meet the ordeal.*]

LORD POVERTY.

[*Introducing* JACK.] Mr. Randolph — correspondent, and art critic of the New York Earth. [JACK *bows.*]

HELEN.

[*Aside.*] Isn't he handsome! [*Sorrowfully.*] And sharing my exile.

JACK RANDOLPH.

[*A handsome young American about twenty.*

self reliant, and full of courage. Exchanges glances with HELEN. *The latter turns aside, to keep from laughing.* JACK *assumes a frigid dignity, looks at painting.*] "Van Elfins Peace", oh yes.

MR. MABY.

You are, no doubt familiar with his work?

JACK.

[*Withouth paying the least attention to* MABY'S *last remark.*] Grand! [*Viewing the picture from another position.*] Water color— [HELEN *nearly swoons.*]

HELEN.

My!

MR. MABY.

Water color?

JACK.

[*Conscious of his awful blunder.*] The water is colored too much, see? [*Pointing to river.*] The reflected tints in the river, are deeper than the color of the clouds.

MR. SMILE.

By Jove, thats so!

HELEN.

[*Relieved at* JACK'S *adroitness, yet fearing another blunder, beckons to Poverty to get him out of the dilemma.*] Oh dear!

LORD POVERTY.

[*Who has been talking to* GOWER, *takes in the situation.*] By the way, gentlemen, the Committees have decided.

ALL.

They have! [*Enters* RUSHFOOT, *with large map, in role, under his arm.*]

RUSHFOOT.

[*A tall, slim, wirey man, about fifty five: has dark, piercing, snapping eyes, smooth face, long thick, black, Indian hair, that's cut strait around, and falls just to his coat collar. Has a habit of projecting his lower lip upwards. When excited, he turns his head with such rapidity, that his hair switches about, and at times, into his face, when he throws it back, over his ears, with a quick, jerky motion. In temper, he gesticulates with great fierceness. Dresses in dark, broad cloth coat, nervously polite, and at times theatrical. Though the features of his face are seldom in repose, he has a kind look and often smiles.*] That's right! After eight hours of dignified, monotonous scrapping, the committees concluded their labors by resolving that Mr. George Maby should stand for parliament. [*Pointing to* MR. MABY.] Gentlemen — behold our future member! Champion of Peace — everlasting Peace, between England and America! Thats right! [*Shakes* MR. MABY'S *hand.*] Dear old England wants peace with the United States. She needs it in her business. [*To* MR. MABY.] This time you're going to be elected. [*Approaching* LORD POVEETY *andshaking his hand.*] Courtland my boy, we'll puil him through.

LORD POVERTY.

Why not?

MR. MABY.

I hope so gentlemen.

RUSHFOOT.

[*To* POVERTY.] If we'd made his last fight he wouldn't have been left. Never! That's right!

LORD POVERTY.

Of course not — but about the votes — he might have lacked a few.

RUSHFOOT.

Not a vote! [*Looking at painting.*] Ten thousand pounds! The man, [*To* LORD POVERTY.] that can buy a fifty thousand dollar picture without knowing how to size its value up has got cheek. In the language of a friend of mine, he is possessed of cheek brass and sublime confidence.

LORD POVERTY.

Fancy!

RUSHFOOT.

Hawkins only beat him by eighty five votes.

GOWER.

The borough has always been close. One man of influence can upset every calculation.

MR. MABY.

[*Leaving* MR. *and* MRS. SMILE, *with whom he has been talking, and approaches* GOWER.] Mr. Gower; — Mr. Rushfoot.

RUSHFOOT.

Delighted sir! [*They shake hands.*]

GOWER.

[*To* RUSHFOOT.] I have a thousand shares of Extension. I'd like to know what you think of the mine.

RUSHFOOT.

[*With slight show of impatience.*] Here's the the last report; read it. (*Hands him report.*)

GOWER.

Oh! thanks! [*To* SMILE.] I want to sell the shares, not to read about the mine. [GOWER *and* SMILE *take seats to the right and examine report.*]

MR. SMILE.

[*To* GOWER.] My wife has a thousand shares.

Lord Poverty has three thousand. [*Punches* GOWER.] Good time to sell.

GOWER.

[*Looks at* SMILE *significantly.*] George Maby will buy my shares or stay at home. [*Enters* OLD MABY.]

OLD MABY.

[*A nervous old man, with long white hair. Active and petulant.*] I'm indignant. [*To* RUSHFOOT.] Some one has hung George Washington's portrait in Devon House; they should have hung him at Yorktown.

LORD POVERTY.

[*Looking at* RUSHFOOT, *as though enjoying* OLD MABY'S *outburst.*] Fancy?

OLD MABY.

And that royal idiot George the Third should have been strung up the same day.

RUSHFOOT.

[*Who observed* POVERTY'S *odd gaze, looks at him in return.*] How about that, Poverty?

LORD POVERTY.

Of course — one of the Dutch chaps — he was an ass, from the cravat up.

OLD MABY.

[*To* LORD POVERTY.] Didn't these two Georges separate the greatest people that ever lived? [*To* RUSHFOOT.] Didn't they commence the fuss?

RUSHFOOT.

[*To* LORD POVERTY.] That's right! Your George started the row, and our George finished it.

OLD MABY.

If it wasn't for those two Georges! [*To* RUSHFOOT.] Say, Rushfoot, you ought to have seen me kick George the Third out of my library. [*To* LORD POVERTY. *In confidence, and nodding his head toward* RUSHFOOT.] They didn't want to separate.

RUSHFOOT.

[*Overhearing* OLD MABY'S *remark. To* OLD MABY.] No. Why my dear man, nearly three-fourths of the signers of the Declaration of Independence, died of broken hearts.

OLD MABY.

[*To* RUSHFOOT.] Say Rushfoot, if we'd lived then!

RUSHFOOT.

Perhaps you did?

OLD MABY.

No I was born in eighteen hundred and twelve

RUSHFOOT.

Eighteen and twelve — we had another scrap with dear old England, that year.

OLD MABY.

[*Anxiously.*] Who came out best?

RUSHFOOT.

It ended in a compromise. [*Looks at* POVERTY *and smiles.*]

OLD MABY,

Good! Do you hear that George!

MR. MABY.

Compromise— Eh? [*Smiling.*]

RUSHFOOT.

[*To* LORD POVERTY.] Thats right! [*Laughing.*]

OLD MABY.

What a lesson!

LORD POVERTY.

It ended in a lesson— of course.

OLD MABY.

A compromise!

LORD POVERTY.

[*Quietly to* OLD MABY.] A compromise — of course. We gave up our ships, and the Yankees stopped their damned fury.

RUSHFOOT.

[*Laughing as he unrolls map of* UNITED STATES *on table. To* POVERTY.] Poverty, here's the Slopper, and here's the Extension —

LORD POVERTY.

I had three thousand Sloppers, among me assets, once. [*Looking at map.*]

RUSHFOOT.

A great mine; it has paid seventeen millions in dividends.

LORD POVERTY.

The dividends from the Slopper kept me on the track for two years; yes, three years among the horses.

GOWER.

[*Joining* POVERTY *and* RUSHFOOT. *To* RUSHFOOT.] You Yankees have such absurd names. Why do you call it the Slopper?

RUSHFOOT.

[*Looking at* GOWER, *as though to reprove his familiarity.*] It's so full of gold, that every time its struck with a pick, the bullion slops over, and falls into the dividend buckets.

GOWER.

Ha, ha, ha — very clever!

MR. SMILE.

[*To* RUSHFOOT.] My wife has a thousand shares.

RUSHFOOT.

[*To* SMILE.] How time flies! Ten years ago — the day your wife graduated from school, I persuaded her to subscribe for one thousand shares. In three months the dividends exceeded the investment.

MR. SMILE.

[*To himself.*] And she never put up a shilling.

GOWER.

Where is the mine?

RUSHFOOT.

In Colorado.

GOWER.

And is that in North America?

RUSHFOOT.

Yes. [HELEN, *who has has been looking at paintings, with* JACK *and* MR. MABY, *laughs.*]

HELEN.

My!

GOWER

[*Pointing to map.*] What's that bit of yellow there?

RUSHFOOT.

New York.

GOWER

Is the Brooklyn bridge in New York?

RUSHFOOT.

Yes.

GOWER

Is Niagara Falls in New York?

RUSHFOOT.

Part of it.

GOWER

I suppose you see the cataract, before you dock?

HELEN.

[*Laughing.*] My!

RUSHFOOT,

From Bloomingdale — yes.

GOWER

Where is Denver?

RUSHFOOT.

In Colorado.

GOWER

Is that far from New York?

RUSHFOOT.

Three days.

GOWER

I mean by the cars.

RUSHFOOT.

By the cars.

GOWER

What makes them go so slow?

RUSHFOOT.

[*In despair.*] They go through Ohio and Patagonia, the adjoining state, on canal boats.

GOWER

Years ago, some English chaps I knew, were making money, in machine ice in Colorado; but finally the Yankees ruined them.

RUSHFOOT.

How?

GOWER

Underselling them; the scamps woundn't have driven me out of the business.

RUSHFOOT.

[*Disgusted.*] There have been bitter ice wars in Colorado. In eighty-six an Englishmann of fabulous wealth, went into that business, and in six months he had the field to himself. He ruined every man in the business.

GOWER

[*Interrupting.*] An Englishman? [*Looking at* RUSHFOOT.] You see he had money. He ruined them. Ha, ha, ha — he had money.

RUSHFOOT.

Yes, all but a Yankee.

GOWER.

A Yankee, how did he help himself?

RUSHFOOT.

He connected the Kennebec River with the Colorado Canal, carried the water over Pikes Peak, above the freezing altitude, by a new system of locks; the whole river went up water, and came down ice. [HELEN *and* JACK *laugh*, MR. MABY *approaches* GOWER.]

GOWER.

[*Astonished.*] You Yankees are clever beggars, at that sort of trick.

MR. MABY.

[*To* GOWER.] By the way, how is Hawkins on arbitration?

GOWER.

He's for arbitration—

MR. SMILE.

And the Nicaragua Canal, or any other canal that unites the two oceans.

GOWER.

That's it.

RUSHFOOT.

[*With deliberation.*] When the Atlantic and Pacific are joined together by the hand of man, it will be by a canal dug, owned and controlled by my countrymen—alone—with the courage and might of the Republic behind them.

MR. SMILE.

We have rights under treaty.

GOWER.

[*To* SMILE.] Have we? Certainly — treaty rights and we'll maintain them. [*To* RUSHFOOT.] Since you Yankees got up this Monroe Doctrine affair there's no putting up with you. What's the thing, anyway?

RUSHFOOT.

The Monroe Doctrine?

GOWER.

Yes.

RUSHFOOT.

A Yankee notice to the governments of the old world, that they can have one half of the earth, and no more, except what they stole, when Uncle Sam wasn't about to prevent the larceny.

LORD POVERTY.

It's the way to slice the bothering old planet up, anyway — why not?

OLD MABY.

It's a compromise. [GOWER *laughs in derision.*]

RUSHFOOT.

[*To* GOWER.] That's right! Its a compromise,

decreed by nature, when she planted the Americans within the protecting circle of her mighty waters, and the men, who think for kings, had better bear that in mind.

OLD MABY.

We must let the South American Republics alone.

MR. SMILE.

Yes, if they behave themselves.

OLD MABY.

Say, Gower, the States are determined. [*Looking at* SMILE.]

GOWER.

We'll have half of the canal anyway.

RUSHFOOT.

Never!

GOWER.

The Yankee bird is a harmless screecher. [OLD MABY *retires in disgust.*]

MR. SMILE.

[*Laughing.*] But look out when the British lion roars!

GOWER.

Say, Smile — a few shots planted along their sea coast —

RUSHFOOT.

[*To* GOWER.] Dont! — dont plant that kind of seed in the States.

GOWER.

Then don't attempt to interfere, with Englands affairs in South America, and give us the canal.

RUSHFOOT.

[*Without paying attention to* GOWER'S *last remark.*] If you do, your country will reap a frightful harvest.

GOWER.

The idea! [*Laughs.*]

RUSHFOOT.

[*See's* MR. MABY *beckoning to him.*] It will be— a mistake. My dear sir, it will terrify the whole white faced race.

LORD POVERTY.

Of course — To say nothing of the Chinese, the niggers — and the rest of the chocolate chaps. [MR. MABY *whispers to* POVERTY. *Enters* OLD MABY.]

OLD MABY.

We'll arbitrate, we've got to arbitrate. It's the cheapest way to build a Canal.

LORD POVERTY.

[*To* RUSHFOOT.] Gower controls, fifty votes.

RUSHFOOT.

The devil! what's to be done?

LORD POVERTY.

I'll take a hand at him.

RUSHFOOT.

Good! fix him — tell him that I'm eloquent on the other side of the question. [*Approaches* MR. MABY, *making apologetic gestures.*]

LORD POVERTY.

[*To* GOWER, *oddly gracious.*] You're quite right; the Yankees must throw the Monroe Doctrine to the dogs.

GOWER.

[*With emphasis.*] I say so.

LORD POVERTY.

If they dont, we'll choke their harbors up with fighting ships. Some day.

GOWER.

The sooner the better; before they're prepared for us.

LORD POVERTY.

If we ever have any trouble with the States the Yankee eagle will take quick flight, when it sees our war ships, with a lion on every deck, tearing up and down the Atlantic coast, knocking the tide about; and the brutes roaring away like blazes.

GOWER.

That's it.

LORD POVERTY.

But about Rushfoot, he's not a bad old chap. He's told me quietly, that England ought to be entitled to a slice now and then, of all the South American countries.

GOWER.

Is it possible?

LORD POVERTY.

Of course — he said in a public speech, in New York, that it was a shame to attempt to check Englands national avarice.

GOWER.

Fancy!

LORD POVERTY.

Of course — he told the President to his face,

that England's larceny, of bits of Venezuela ought to be encouraged.

GOWER.

He's right.

LORD POVERTY.

That England's grab was only the swipe of a higher civilization.

GOWER.

What did the President say?

LORD POVERTY.

[*Pronounced wink.*] That's all.

GOWER.

[*Winks in return, clutches* POVERTY'S *arm, and nods significantly.*] That's it!

RUSHFOOT.

[*Who has been watching* POVERTY *and* GOWER.] Gentlemen — Why see! America turned Venezuela down. Blood is thicker than water; same ancestry, same language.

LORD POVERTY.

Of course — we lie in the same vernacular — to be sure.

RUSHPOOT.

[*To* GOWER.] We have to put on national side, now and then — to stand the Spaniards off. But England — dear old England — [*Puts his arms around* LORD POVERTY'S *and* GOWER'S *neck and whispers.*] Olney and Salisbury understood each other. When arbitration becomes a fact, [*To* LORD POVERTY.] what do you suppose we'll do?

LORD POVERTY.

Yes, you told me — of course. [*To* GOWER.] Both countries are going down to Venezuela and knock the tar — [*To* RUSHFOOT.] Did Cleveland say tar? [RUSHFOOT *nods assent.* knock the tar out of the beggars.

RUSHFOOT.

[*To* GOWER.] Sure! That's right!

LORD POVERTY.

England is to take one half of the country—

RUSHFOOT.

And Uncle Sam what's left.

LORD POVERTY.

Yes — of course. Carve the damn country in two — Why not? [*Noise without.*]

MR. MABY.

[*Going to window.*] Another commotion! what does it all mean?

HELEN.

[*Rushing to the window.*] Its a parade!

MR. MABY.

Of the Arbitration League. [*Cheers for* MABY *and* ARBITRATION *are heard from the street.*]

RUSHFOOT.

[*Who has joined* HELEN.] They see you George! They see you! [*Enters* OLD MABY *excited,*]

OLD MABY.

The Arbitration League is marching on Devon House.

HELEN.

They've stopped! Signior Sirao is talking with their leader.

RUSHFOOT.

He's asking them in. [*Music*— "RULE BRITANNIA."

OLD MABY.

[*Wildly.*] The fight is on! Hawkins wont be in it, this time! [*Enter members of the parade, bearing large transparency. They crowd about the left entrance. The leader advances, and bows to* MR. MABY. *On the transparency is a representation of* JOHN BULL, *stepping from a boat to shore.* UNCLE SAM *receiving him, with open arms, and broad smile.*]

RUSHFOOT.

[*Pointing to transparency.*] That's right! Dear old Bull should know more of us; he'd be wiser.

OLD MABY.

That's what arbitration means! [*Transparency*

is turned. UNCLE SAM *is seen, standing in a boat, that's just touching the shores of England.* JOHN BULL, *on land, waiting to receive him. Surrounding the latter, are a number of dukes, and lords with coronets, on their heads, and wearing other insignia of exalted rank. In the boat with* UNCLE SAM *are numberless young and old women holding bags of money in their hands, all anxious to get ashore. One fat widow is jumping into the water. Music from outer hall —* "YANKEE DOODLE".]

RUSHFOOT.

[*To* LORD POVERTY.] My dear boy! That's the favorite tune of the "Goddess of Liberty", In my country, those strains elevate the spirits. of the rich, and poor, high and low, to the same exalted summit of human merriment.

OLD MABY.

[*Looking at transparency.*] There's more arbitration. [*Laughs. Transparency is turned,* UNCLE SAM *and* JOHN BULL, *arm in arm, hats on back of their heads, doing the town. Music —* "WE WONT GO HOME" *until morning.*]

[*Looking at transparency.*] No wonder! The dear old boys are only celebrating their reunion. Oh — those two Georges!

LEADER.

[*Bowing and advancing.* To MR. MABY.] The decision of the general and local committees has so aroused myself, and other members of the International Arbitration League, that we've hastened, with scant preparation, to pledge to you our support in the coming election for Parliament. [*Bows and steps back.*]

MR. MABY.

[*Bowing.*] Gentlemen, I thank you for these evidences of friendship. [*Bows.*]

VOICE.

Three cheers for Maby! [*Cheers.*]

MR. MABY.

Gentlemen, I have chosen Lord Poverty and

Mr. Rushfoot, two members of you league, to conduct my campaign. [*Bows.*]

VOICE.

Lord Poverty! Speech! Speech!

VOICE.

Speech! Speech! [RUSHFOOT *and* OLD MABY *force* LORD POVERTY *upon a chair.* PARADERS *crowd around entrance.*]

LORD POVERTY.

Gentlemen. [*Bowing.*] To be sure — send Maby away to Parliament — to get arbitration with the States. Why not? The Yankee and the Britisher have been handed down in natural order — from the same mothers. Why not? We've the same tongue — of course; but we wag it away at each other, too much. We must arbitrate, not fight. Whats the use of relations, shooting, jabbing and yelling away at each other like madmen — there's no sense in it. I'm through, why not? [*Bowing.*]

RUSHFOOT.

Three cheers for the best lord in Burks Peerage! Lord Courtland Poverty! [*Cheers - Music* "HE'S A JOLLY GOOD FELLOW". *Paraders retiring —* LORD POVERTY *remains on chair, waving handkerchief.* RUSHFOOT, *bowing with sweeping gestures, as the curtain falls.*]

END OF THE FIRST ACT.

THE SECOND ACT.

One week has elapsed between the first and second act.

The Scene is the large foyer hall of DEVON HOUSE, DORCHESTER OAKS, residence of MR. GEORGE MABY. At the back, and between the right, and left entrances are two wide stair cases, ascending in segmental curves to a square landing, eight feet from the floor. The stairs and landing have heavy carved balustrades, Between the stairs is a curved recess, in which rests, on a large easel, "VAN ELFIN'S PEACE". The painting stands perpendicularly. The top of the gilt frame is held by wooden cross piece, to prevent it from falling forward. Attached to the easel, is a frame, elevated above the painting, and with cross bar, upon which are gas jets, with reflectors, to illuminate the canvas, as in the first act. The left entrance leads into interior hall, with door leading, it's supposed, to main front vestibule hall. The right entrance leads into another interior hall, with door leading, its supposed, to rear, main entrance of house. On the left is a library with arched pillared entrance. Immediately opposite the library on the right is the drawing room, with entrance same as library. Telephone on the wall.

OLD MABY is walking up and down the stage. GOWER is awaiting the arrival of MR. GEORGE MABY. JACK is reading bulletins, that are brought by MESSENGER, from the library. HELEN, in street costume, stands to the right near JACK, hearing the latest election news, and now and then, signaling to him her contempt for GOWER. TAYLOR and SALLY are busy clearing away electioneering literature etc. etc. The whole Scene bespeaks bustle and excitement.

OLD MABY.

[To JACK, who has just finished reading bulletin.] Read that again, young man!

JACK.

[*Reads.*] "A heavy vote has been cast throughout the borough. Hawkins predicts his own election, by a majority of from one hundred and fifty to two hundred."

OLD MABY.

Hawkins predicts! [*Scornfully.*] The assumptive ass! [*Looking at* GOWER.] Eh? [*Enters* MESSENGER *from library with bulletin; hands it to* JACK. MESSENGER *retires.*]

JACK.

Another bulletin! [*Reads.*] "Tis said that the Gover faction [GOWER *looks difiantly.*] are holding off. A tally of the votes cast up to this writing, gives Hawkins a majority of seventy five.

GOWER.

Gower faction! [*Snappishly.*] I don't control any bodys vote, but my own. [*Aside.*] Except forty five. [*To* OLD MABY *with affected dignity,*] I have called sir, to see Mr. George Maby.

OLD MABY.

[*Aside.*] If he wasn't in this house. [*To* GOWER.] He may be here in one minute, sir, or not for an hour, sir — an hour, sir. [*Enters* MESSENGER; *hands Jack bulletin.* MESSENGER *retires.*]

JACK.

[*Reads.*] "Tis said that Maby will lose fifty votes on account of the meet. The hunt is the largest of the season."

OLD MABY.

[*Violently kicking a chair.*] Damn the hunt!

HELEN.

[*Indignantly.*] The idea! Hunt today! [*Kicks chair, hurts her foot.* JACK *turns around, and laughs, to himself, at* HELEN'S *mishap.* HELEN *scowls at* JACK. *Enters* MESSENGER. MESSENGER *retires.*]

JACK.

[*Continuing to read.* HELEN *nurses her injured foot.*] "Five members of the Gower faction openly avow their intentions of voting for Hawkins, as a rebuke to the audacious intermeddling in English politics, of the Devon House Yankees, so called."

OLD MABY.

[*To* SALLY.] Here you new girl, where is Mrs. Maby?

SALLY

Hout sir.

OLD MABY

[*To* TAYLOR.] Where is Mr. Rushfoot?

TAYLOR.

'E went to the polls with 'is lordship, sir.

OLD MABY.

[*Petulantly.*] Every one out! [*Goes to left entrance.*] Devon House Yankees! [TAYLOR *and* SALLY *retire, carrying bundless of electioneering literature.* OLD MABY *looks at* GOWER *and then at* JACK. *Approaches latter. To* JACK.] You're the art chap.

JACK.

Yes sir.

OLD MABY.

A Yankee?

JACK.

Yes sir.

OLD MABY.

Devon House is yours! [*To* HELEN.] Make it pleasant for this young man.

HELEN.

[*Suppressing a smile.*] I shall try.

JACK.

[*To* OLD MABY.] Thank you! [*To* HELEN.] Miss Rushfoot, you are very kind. [*Bowing.*]

OLD MABY.

[*Goes to left entrance.*] Devon House Yankees! [*Looks at* GOWER *exit.*]

GOWER.

[*Looking after* OLD MABY.] Eh? [*Laughs.*

Takes out his watch.] The old gentlemen is excited.

JACK.

[*To* HELEN.] Let's guy the duffer.

HELEN.

Yes. I despise him!

GOWER.

[*Approaching* JACK *in a patronizing manner.*] Have you been long in England, young man?

JACK.

Ten days.

GOWER.

In London?

JACK.

Eight days.

GOWER.

You've seen the Tower?

JACK.

The Eiffle Tower?

GOWER.

No? the London Tower,

JACK.

Is that in England?

GOWER.

Where else could it be! You've seen Westminster?

JACK.

Westminster? Westminster?

GOWER.

The Abbey?

JACK.

Oh yes! that big church on the banks of the — — [*To* HELEN·] Do you know Miss Rushfoot, that I can never think of the name of that river?

GOWER.

The Thames — the Thames. [*With a crushing look.*] Havn't you ever studied geography?

JACK.

I'm an authority in my country, on geograyhical matters.

GOWER.

You've studied English geography, havn't you?

JACK.

[*Reflecting.*] Really, I've forgotten. [*To* HELEN.] Did you, Miss Rushfoot?

HELEN.

Why yes, Mr. Randolpf. Don't you remember? — England comes in among the islands.

JACK.

So it does! [*Repeating.*] Iceland, Madagascar, Ireland —

HELEN.

[*Interrupting.*] Long Island —

JACK.

And then England.

HELEN.

No, no! Staten Island comes next!

JACK.

Oh yes! Staten Island — Fire Island —

HELEN.

Coney Island —

JACK.

And then England. That's it! [*Looking at* GOWER.]

GOWER.

[*In a rage,*] Such ignorance! The idea! Bah! [*Rushes off stage.*]

JACK.

[*Looking after* GOWER.] Ha — ha — ha, his heart is broken. [*Enters* MESSENGER *with bulletin.* JACK *looks at it and puts it on table,* MESSENGER *retires.*]

HELEN.

[*Laughing.*] Wasn't it fun!

JACK.

[*Takes a seat, catches* HELEN'S *hands, who stands back of his chair.*] Entertain me.]*Trying gently to pull her head down to kiss her.*]

HELEN.

[*With mock dignity.*] I fear — dear sir — I cant.

JACK.

[*Baffled in his efforts to kiss her.*] I'm surprised that you should throw away, an opportunity so auspicious. [*Closing his eyes and affecting to sleep.*]

HELEN.

To entertain an art critic, is no trifling task.

JACK.

[*Jumping up.*] Stop! stop! it's annoying. [*Affecting to be hurt, then kisses her.*]

HELEN.

[*Without moving, and closing her eyes for a moment to give* JACK *another chance.*] You are,

I assume quite familiar with the works of the great Van Elfin. [*Imitating* MR. MABY.]

JACK.

Stop, stop!

HELEN.

[*Imitating* JACK.] "Water color"!

JACK.

Now Helen! — But I'm ready for the next ordeal. I sat up all night, writing out speeches on art. [*Shows* HELEN *writing on his cuffs.*]

HELEN.

[*Paying no attention to what* JACK *says and pointing.*] "The tints from the reflected waters are" — [*Imitating* JACK.]

JACK.

[*Approaching* HELEN.] Are not half as beautiful as the tints on your cheeks. [*Kisses her.*]

HELEN.

Now Jack, *you* stop! [*Pouting.*] I'll remember that.

JACK.

Remember it! I should say so! I'm four ahead of you now.

HELEN.

You're not!

JACK.

I am! [*Holding up four fingers.*]

HELEN.

Only three. [*Holding up three fingers.*]

JACK.

Four!

HELEN.

Three! [*Enters* SALLY.[

SALLY

Madame 'as just returned; she wants your field glasses' hif you please.

HELEN.

Where is Mrs. Maby?

SALLY

Going hup hinto the Cupola.

HELEN.

Cupola?

SALLY

Yes Miss 'Elen, to watch the 'ounds. The fox his haleading them, back hof the horchard beyond the 'ill. [HELEN *hurries to left entrance, is about to retire.*]

JACK.

Helen!

HELEN.

What is it?

JACK.

Hurry back and pay your debts.

HELEN.

You awful boy! [*Exit* HELEN.]

JACK.

[*Looking after* HELEN.] She's the finest girl in *this* world. [*Enters* OLD MABY.]

OLD MABY.

[*Looking about.*] Gower gone?

JACK.

Yes sir.

OLD MABY.

"Good riddance bad rubbish!"

JACK.

Mr. Maby, who are the Gower people?

OLD MABY.

[*With emphasis.*] Cringing, beggarly wretches, whose business is at the mercy of the usurious and exacting old tyrant.

JACK.

[*Taking last bulletin from table.*] This last bulletin prompted the inquiry. [*Reads.* "The Gower faction have not yet voted. Their action is not understood."

OLD MABY.

[*Inquiringly.*] What are they waiting for?

JACK.

They're fishing.

OLD MABY.

Fishing?

JACK.

Yes.

OLD MABY,

For what?

JACK.

For soap, — money.

OLD MABY.

[*Looking at* JACK.] That's it! [*After reflection, to himself.*] Where in the devil is George? [*Hurries to left entrance, stands, looks at* JACK.] He has wisdom beyond his years. [JACK *pulls out a segar and looks at it.*] "Fishing for soap." [*Returns. — Takes* JACK *by the arm.*] Do you smoke?

JACK.

Too much — I fear.

OLD MABY.

Come! join me in a segar.

JACK.

Thank you! I'm good for three.

OLD MABY.

[*Looking at* JACK.] Fishing for soap. [*Laughs and then becomes serious.*] They dont do that sort of thing in England.

JACK.

Certainly not! Of course not — not in England.

OLD MABY.

[*Looking at* JACK.] Only in America. [*Laughs. Exeunt* OLD MABY *and* JACK. *Loud happy peals of laughter heard in the vestibule hall. Enter* HELEN *and* MISS EFFIE REVERE, *the latter still laughing*, HELEN *smiling.*]

HELEN.

What did Lord Poverty say?

EFFIE.

[*A beautiful young woman, about nineteen. Richly, though modestly dressed. Dark brown hair, large eyes, and gentle manner. Has a confiding disposition, happy nature and given to paroxysms of laughter.*] Oh dear! [*Laughs.*] I begin to think, that Lord Poverty has got a heart! [*Laughs.*]

HELEN.

[*Smiling.*] How I like to hear you laugh!

EFFIE.

Really? I'm ashamed of myself, but I can't help it. It was so funny. Didn't you hear, what he asked me?

HELEN.

No. I saw you coming from the window just as I was sending Sally to the cupola. I didn't reach the walk in time.

EFFIE.

As the groom was leading his horse away, I

remarked that it was chilly. Lord Poverty looked at me, [*Laughing.*] scrutinized my dress and then asked, if I had plenty of jackets [*Laughs*, HELEN *joins her.*] and — and strong — [*Laughs.*] strong clothes under my gown.

HELEN.

Plenty of jackets? [*Laughs.*]

EFFIE.

Strong clothes! [*Laughs.*] Oh, so funny!

HELEN.

He calls you Maloney, doesn't he?

EFFIE.

Yes. [*Laughing.*] Thats funny too. Last summer, the day I graduated, his lordship, sent me a box of flowers, directing it to Miss Effie Lillian Maloney Revere. How the girls did laugh!

HELEN.

Isn't that one of your names?

EFFIE.

[*Laughing.*] No! not Maloney — Malomey. After my return from school, he met me one afternoon near the chapel and said. "By the way, Maloney, don't you find it awkward knocking about without a brother?" [*Laughs.*] Knocking about! I told him that I often wished I could recall my brother from above. "He'd never forgive you." he replied. "Up there, he's got nothing to do, but to see God and fly around; down here, he'd have to commence dodging the brimstone chap, all over again." Since that day, [*Sorrowfully.*] I have never wished to recall my brother from Heaven. A rugged sermon! — I mustn't think. Well! Finally, on leaving me, he said. "Maloney I'll keep a brother's eye on you." You see, I'm not quite alone in the world.

HELEN.

Do you think it's nice to have a brother? I don't mean a real brother — one that tells you to shut up, and things like that, but a brother that isn't a brother — the kind that falls in love with you.

EFFIE.

I'm not sure that I do.

HELEN.

Jack commenced with me that way.

EFFIE.

He did?

HELEN.

Yes — but the brother business didn't last three days. Your's has lasted longer, hasn't it?

EFFIE.

Laughing.] Yes — five months.

HELEN.

That's too long. Why! I would have died if Jack had kept up that nonsense a day longer

EFFIE.

You're in love. [*Looking at* HELEN.]

HELEN.

And so are —

EFFIE.

No. I think not, I don't know — [*Shaking her head.*]

HELEN.

You ought to be, it's so nice.

EFFIE.

[*Laughing.*] I never expect to be.

HELEN.

[*Sorrowfully.*] Poor girl.

EFFIE.

Do you pity me?

HELEN.

Do fall in love, please! We'll just own this town.

EFFIE.

[*Laughing.*] With whom?

HELEN.

Lord Poverty, of course!

EFFIE.

[*Seriously.*] I don't dare to; I never met him until last summer.

HELEN.

That don't count. I fell in love with Jack the very first time I saw him.

EFFIE.

He is absolutely without sentiment. [*Looks at* HELEN.] Why! here I am telling you —

HELEN.

[*Interrupting.*] I know everything.

EFFIE

[*Surprised*] Who told you?

HELEN.

Lord Poverty.

EFFIE.

[*Laughing.*] He says, he loves me, — [*Seriously.*] but he doesn't know the meaning of the word.

HELEN.

He hasn't much sentiment, I admit; but you might rouse him —

EFFIE.

As Lord Poverty has made a confidante of you, I'll do the same. [*Earnestly.*] I wouldn't promise to become his wife, if he had the sentiment of a poet.

HELEN.

I'm so sorry! A pretty girl like you ought to be in love anyway. I'd go mad, if I didn't love Jack.

EFFIE.

You dear child!

HELEN.

[*Sighing.*] It takes all kinds of people to make a world.

EFFIE.

[*Putting her arms around* HELEN.] Am I so very odd?

HELEN.

[*Nods.*] Yes — throwing away a good thing — that's what Jack calls it.

EFFIE.

[*Looking at* HELEN. *Seriously.*] Let me tell you a story. A tiny girl; an orphan, scarcely ten, lived in Colorado with her brother, twelve years older. Then he was called. Without relatives to care for her she would have — well — died, I suppose; but for a young Englishman, her brother's friend. He caused her to be sent to England, cared for — and educated.

HELEN.

[*Seriously.*] The little girl wasn't you, was it, Effie?

EFFIE.

Yes.

HELEN.

How noble of him. [*Earnestly.*] What is his name?

EFFIE.

Bruce Buckingham.

HELEN.

Oh, I want to meet him!

EFFIE.

I have seen him but twice, and that was in Colorado.

HELEN.

Where is he?

EFFIE.

In India.

HELEN.

Is he nice looking?

EFFIE.

I scarcely remember.

HELEN.

You've got his photograph?

EFFIE.

No. I never heard from him directly until my eighteenth year. Then I got my first letter; I answered it in a flood of tears, and sent him my photograph. Then came another letter from

India, and another, and they continued to come until eleven months ago. In his last letter, he asked me not to marry, or promise to marry without his consent. Could you, under these circumstances, give your heart to the first man who asked it?

HELEN.

If the first man was Jack, I would. Where is Mr. Buckingham now?

EFFIE.

Somewhere in India. He said, in his last letter, that I wouldn't hear from him for a year or more.

HELEN.

Was he fond of your brother?

EFFIE.

Very. The first time my brother met him was in Selida. Some cow-boys had insulted him. My brother seeing that he was a stranger took sides with him; revolvers were drawn and some one would have been killed, had they persisted in their insults. [*Enters* TAYLOR.]

TAYLOR.

[*Excited.*] Hif you please, Miss Helen, the 'unt his hover, the 'ounds, hand whips his returning to the kennels.

HELEN.

[*To* EFFIE.] My! Let us go up in the Cupola, to make sure. It will be fun.

EFFIE.

Yes, splendid! [*Exeunt* HELEN *and* EFFIE. TAYLOR *retires. Enter* MRS. SMILE *and* MRS. MABY.]

MRS. MABY.

I am glad to see you, Lizzie.

MRS. SMILE.

How stupid it was of Mr. Smile to have appointed a meet for today.

MRS. MABY.

Scold him, for me.

MRS. SMILE.

You'll be glad when the election is over, especially the celebration.

MRS. MABY.

Yes — especially the latter.

MRS. SMILE.

I trust nothing will happen.

MRS. MABY.

It would kill me.

MRS. SMILE.

You are awfully sensitive, I know.

MRS. MABY.

So far we've been fortunate — except one thing, Signior Sirao left yesterday for Italy.

MRS. SMILE.

[*Surprised.*] Signior Sirao gone?

MRS. MABY.

Paintings and all.

MRS. SMILE.

How unfortunate!

MRS. MABY.

He took offence, we fancy, because our painting was taken here without consulting him. In fact without his knowledge.

MRS. SMILE.

Who's to hang the—

MRS. MABY.

[*Interrupting.*] I thought of asking Mr. Randolph, to direct the hanging.

MRS. SMILE.

The art critic?

MRS. MABY.

Yes. [*Enters* JACK *with note book in hand, on seeing the ladies he bows and attempts to retire.*]

MRS. MABY.

Mr. Randolph, I was about saying, that we venture to hope for a suggestion from you, when we hang our painting at the League Headquarters.

JACK.

Command me, madame.

MRS. SMILE.

[*To* MRS. MABY.] Isn't it very nice of Mr. Randolph. [*Enters* HELEN *and* EFFIE.]

HELEN.

[*To* EFFIE.] Let us wait. I'm awfully nervous.

MRS. MABY.

Rely upon it Mr. Randolph, [*Laughing*.] we shall press your talents into service. [JACK *bows*.]

HELEN.

[*To* EFFIE.] Isn't he graceful, and how handsome! I wish Jack had assumed some other role — I'm afraid.

JACK.

[*To* MRS. MABY.] You admire the sublimities of the canvas, madame.

MRS. MABY.

Yes — yet I fear, that one like yourself, skilled in the beauties and subtile refinements of high art, will marvel, when I confess, that though passionately fond of the masters, I can't tell why.

JACK.

The masters painted up — [*Looking at his cuff.*] painted up —

HELEN.

[*Alarmed.*] Any other role! [*To herself.*]

JACK.

Not only to meet the severe exactions of the connoisseur, but [*Looking at cuff.*] down again, to accommodate the artistic incapacities of a lady like — yourself — I mean —

MRS. MABY.

[*Laughing.*] Like me. But how I admire Ruben!

HELEN.

[*To* EFFIE.] That was great, but awfully

impudent. My! [*Puts her hands to her mouth to stifle her merriment.*]

JACK.

[*Rests right elbow on chair, the cuff of other arm exposed. Affects a dreamy faraway look.*] Rubens! Rubens! Look upon a Ruben the canvas vanishes, you behold instead, but an opening in the mighty gate, that swings in the portals of the past. Through the forbidden entrance, the living catch glimpses of men and women, things and affairs, that the hand of Ruben has rescued from the shades of the forgotten. The works of the masters, are but living fragments of the dead past.

MRS. MABY.

Beautiful!

MRS. SMILE.

Grand!

HELEN.

[*Astonished.*] Who told Jack that? [*Enters* OLD MABY.]

OLD MABY.

[*Excited.*] Where in the — [*Seeing the ladies.*] on earth, is George?

MRS. MABY.

[*To* OLD MABY.] I got this letter from him half an hour ago.

OLD MABY.

[*Reads.*] "Things are looking nasty in Chapel Parish. Send by bearer, package in upper right hand drawer of safe." [*Looking at* MRS. MABY.] That was soap. Did you send it?

MRS. MABY.

Soap?

OLD MABY.

Yes, soap. [*Points to letter and reads.*] "Things are looking nasty in Chapel Parish." Don't you see? [*Confidentially.*] He wanted soap to wash the dirty consciences of the Gower gang.

MRS. MABY.

It was his check book on the London Bank.

OLD MABY.

[*Laughing and looking at* MRS. MABY.] That wasn't soap! Oh no! 'twas sopolio. [*Laughs.*] The scoundrels! [MRS. MABY *joins* MRS. SMILE *and both retire to the drawing room   Enters* MESSENGER *with bulletin.*]

OLD MABY.

[*Approaching* JACK.] What is it? [MESSENGER *retires.*]

JACK.

[*Reads.*] "Having received pledges from the liberal candidate, that he would support the 'One Man, One Vote' bill, the Gower faction have voted for Maby to a man."

OLD MABY.

[*Looking at* JACK.] Young man, 'twas pledges, not soap they wanted. [JACK *looks at* OLD MABY *with a droll smile.*] He doesn't belive it — he knows too much. [*To himself.*]

MRS. MABY.

[*To* OLD MABY *from drawing room entrance.*] Then George will win!

OLD MABY.

Win—, yes.

HELEN.

[*To* EFFIE.] I'sn't that glorious! [*Enters* MESSENGER *with bulletin.* MESSENGER *retires.*]

JACK.

[*Reads.*] "It is admitted by all, that the election turns upon the vote of Chapel Parish. The situation there is alarming. Fifty seven liberal members are at the hunt. Rushfoot was last seen, riding in the direction of the run."

HELEN.

But the hunt is over! [*Telephone rings.*]

OLD MABY.

[*Going to telephone.*] Well? [*Listens repeats.*] "Rushfoot is now heading the recreant liberals to the polls." Good! [*Hangs phone.*] Where is Hawkins now? Hurrah—!

HELEN.

Hurrah! Our side wins! [*Enters* TAYLOR.]

TAYLOR.

[*To* OLD MABY.] Ha foreign looking chap sir, 'as been loitering habout the hentrance of the garden, hall day sir.

OLD MABY.

What does he want?

TAYLOR.

'E wants nothing that Hi know hof sir, 'E's been achasing hof the Italian boy, sir.

MRS. MABY.

[*From drawing room entrance.*] Maxey here?

TAYLOR.

Yes marm. E's been loitering habout habit too, marm.

OLD MABY.

Drive them away!

MRS. MABY.

[*Entering from drawing room. To* OLD MABY]

Let me attend to the matter. [*To* MRS. SMILE.] I'll have to leave you for a moment. [*To* TAYLOR.] Find Maxey. [TAYLOR *retires*.] The boy left! I don't understand it! [*Exit* MRS. MABY.]

OLD MABY.

[*Annoyed.*] Some mendicant. [*Exit* OLD MABY.]

HELEN.

[*Who has been talking to* JACK *and* EFFIE. *To* EFFIE.] Wouldn't you like to?

EFFIE.

If it isn't too dark, your lawn is so beautiful.

HELEN.

[*To* JACK.] Come, Mr. Randolph, we're going on the lawn. Mrs. Smile will excuse us.

MRS. SMILE.

Certainly. [*Exeunt* HELEN, JACK *and* EFFIE.]

MRS. SMILE.

[*Looking about her with gleaming eyes.*]

Signor Sirao gone! What a sensation. This will be the story. [*Laughs.*] "To humor a Yankee wife, who longed to breath the air of a higher social altitude, an Englishman pays ten thousand pounds for a piece of counterfeit art; and to seek royal favor, presents his vulgar purchase to a society of sentimentalists, suffering from yankeesmite. His Royal Highness, the Prince of Wales, is asked to honor the occasion by making the presentation speech." It's nauseating — [*Laughs.*] the explosion that will follow, will rouse such a whirl-wind of indignation throughout England, that the Maby's will be blown into the very crevices of social obscurity. [*Looking about her again.*] Maby may win in spite of the hunt — no matter. The greater the height, the greater the fall. [*Reflecting.*] I don't like this Maxey business; they musn't know the truth, it would spoil my game. I will find him myself. [*Exit* MRS. SMILE. *Enter* HELEN *and* JACK.]

HELEN.

I didn't know it was so dark. Why don't Effie come?

JACK.

[*Dropping in chair.*] She stopped to talk with Lord Poverty.

HELEN.

[*Standing behind* JACK *and putting her arms on his shoulders.*] Jack, I'm proud of you. Oh, how I long for a swing!

JACK.

Swing?

HELEN.

Yes— on the "gate that swings in the portals the past." [*Laugh.* JACK *kisses* HELEN'S *hand. She slaps him gently on the cheek.*]

JACK.

That's no love pat.

HELEN.

Then stop!

JACK.

I was only making it six.

HELEN.

[*Looking about.*] I don't want five. [BENSON *appears.* HELEN *kisses him.*] Take it back, [*Sees* BENSON.] Oh! [*Rolling up her eyes.*] As I was saying, dear cousin.

JACK.

Don't cousin me. [HELEN *trys to attract* JACK'S *attention, to* BENSON, *but failing she puts her hand over his mouth.*]

HELEN.

[*To* JACK.] Benson!

JACK.

The cat! [JACK *turns his head sees* BENSON, *jumps up.*] Pardon me. [*Bowing.*]

HELEN.

[*Looking at* BENSON.] Oh. I'm so pleased to see you. [*Enters* POVERTY, BENSON *seaches in her pocket for letter.* POVERTY *stands with hand extended to receive it.*]

HELEN.

[*Remembering her promise.*] Go Jack, into the drawing room, quick! [*Laughing.*] Don't remain here. [*Takes him by the arm.*] Go. "Her Last Dupe" is a splendid picture. Look at it!

JACK.

[*Goes reluctantly.*] This is nice!

HELEN.

[*Goes to* POVERTY.] Courtland dear! [*Kisses him.*]

JACK.

[*Standing in entrance of drawing room.*] Courtland dear! [*Reenters hall, takes his hat from table, rushes toward right entrance.*] "Her Last Dupe." [*Exit* JACK.]

HELEN.

Jack, Jack, come back! [*Laughing. Exit* HELEN.]

POVERTY.

Of course. [*Takes letter from* BENSON.] This is for—

BENSON.

Your lordship. [BOWING. *Goes to left entrance. Bows again. Exit* BENSON.]

POVERTY.

[*Looking at left entrance at though expecting some one.*] I told her to come in out of the dampness. [*Enters* EFFIE.]

EFFIE.

Where did Helen go?

POVERTY.

After the critic.

EFFIE.

Oh yes, Mr. Randolph.

POVERTY.

The grass is full of water.

EFFIE.

It isn't damp, but its dark. [*Looking at her shoes.*]

POVERTY.

You've got a fine look on today. Maloney.

EFFIE.

[*Smiling.*] Thank you; how is your Lordship?

POVERTY.

A bit sentimental.

EFFIE.

Sentimental!

POVERTY.

I think so — I'm not sure.

EFFIE.

You! [*Laughs.*]

POVERTY.

Why not? By the way, do you remember that bit of rhyming stuff, about a chap that went growling about, longing to meet another life?

EFFIE.

Another life?

POVERTY.

Another girl— no— not another one, but the right one.

EFFIE.

[*Inquiringly.*] "There's another life I long to meet?"

POVERTY.

That's it.

EFFIE.

"There's another life I long to meet. Without which life, my life incomplete."

POVERTY.

Clever, very clever. I've been rapping the thing about on me tongue's end all day, but when I saw you I forgot it. What became of the wretch? Did he ever overtake her? [*Looking at* EFFIE.] Of course— to be sure.

EFFIE.

Perhaps.

POVERTY.

"Without which life, my life is incomplete."

[*Approaching* EFFIE.] I know a chap, a good enough chap too, who wants to take your life.

EFFIE.

Mine?

POVERTY.

And fill it with nonsense, and flowers and bonnets, and a horse or two. He hasn't money, but I think he can throw in the horses.

EFFIE.

Your friend ought not to marry without money.

POVERTY.

Why not?

EFFIE.

The responsibilities following marriage—

POVERTY.

[*Looking at* EFFIE.] The responsibilities?

EFFIE.

Yes.

POVERTY.

Oh them things — they'll be provided for. The young Povertys always start rich. You see, I'm the chap I'm talking about.

EFFIE.

You! [*Laughing.*]

POVERTY.

Why not?

EFFIE.

You'll have plenty of money some day.

POVERTY.

I'm going to let the two thousand a year go.

EFFIE.

I dont understand you?

POVERTY.

You see, me aunt is to leave me two thousand a year, provided I marry money. I'm against marrying the stuff. I want *you*.

EFFIE.

[*Laughing.*] Do you really care for me?

POVERTY.

Why not?

EFFIE.

[*Seriously.*] You only think so.

POVERTY.

I'm a bad hand at this business.

EFFIE.

[*To herself.*] Really, he loves me. [*To* POVERTY.] Don't, don't imperil your future on my account. Make no sacrifice for me, I'm not worthy of it.

POVERTY.

You see, Maloney, I'm tired of tricking me aunt. [*Enters* OLD MABY *from right entrance excited.*]

OLD MABY.

[*To* POVERTY.] You speak Italian?

POVERTY.

Why not?

OLD MABY.

Come with me!

POVERTY.

Of course.

OLD MABY.

The Italian tramp and the boy Maxey are raising the devil! [*Goes to right entrance. Exeunt* POVERTY *and* OLD MABY.]

EFFIE.

Poor Lord Poverty. Oh dear! [*Enters* SALLY.]

SALLY

Madame wants to 'ave you join 'er, hin the music room, hif you please.

EFFIE.

Right away. [*Exit* EFFIE. SALLY *retires. Enter* MR. *and* MRS. SMILE.]

MRS. SMILE.

[*Excited.*] Well!

MR. SMILE.

The hunt was broken up; Rushfoot outwitted us.

MRS. SMILE.

How?

MR. SMILE.

By jove, I don't know.

MRS. SMILE.

Well!

MR. SMILE.

Don't be impatient, I will give you the facts.

MRS. SMILE.

That's what I want!

MR. SMILE.

When nearing the Monk Well, Rushfoot came dashing after us, at a fearful pace. He passed us in an instant, rushing in among the hounds.

I thought he would trample the bellowing brutes. to death. On he plunged, outstripping the foremost leader of the pack. When rounding the road, that turns to the Giant oak he fell. The impetus of his mad dash was so great, that it swung his body around the bend out of view. Major Bradford and I hurried to the spot, expecting to find him badly hurt, but there he was, sitting on his horse laughing. Bradford asked if his fall was serious, Rushfoot replied that he didn't fall and continued to laugh. This nettled Bradford, who doesn't like the Yankees, you know, and he retorted that the tongue of many a man had deceived him, but that his own eye sight never had. Rushfoot remarked with provoking coolness, that he need'nt boast of his sight, for he owned a mule once, that could outhsight him. When Bradford returned to the club, he wrote a letter to Rushfoot, demanding an apology, or satisfaction.

MRS. SMILE.

Is it possible? This is news indeed!

MR. SMILE.

It's an odd fact, that the hounds on reaching the spot, where Rushfoot fell, lost the scent, and the whips called them off.

MRS. SMILE.

If the nineteenth passes, without more than one scandal, then I don't read the signs. [*Enters* HELEN, *followed by* MR. MABY, MRS. MABY *and* TAYLOR.]

MRS. MABY.

[*To* TAYLOR.] What's the trouble?

TAYLOR.

[*Out of breath.*] The foreign chap caught Maxey and 'e beat 'im hover the 'ead marm.

MR. MABY.

[*To* TAYLOR.] The man who's been loitering about all day?

TAYLOR.

Yes sir. 'Ed 'ave killed 'im, hif hit 'adn't been for Mr. Randolph. [*Enter* JACK, POVERTY *and* OLD MABY.]

OLD MABY.

The boy insensible! [MRS. MABY *alarmed*, POVERTY *whispers to her. They look toward painting.*]

MRS. MABY.

Impossible! [*Almost faints.*]

MR. MABY.

[*To* TAYLOR.] Who is this tramp!

TAYLOR.

The hartist sir.

MRS. MABY.

Signor Sirao.

TAYLOR.

Yes, madame.

MR. MABY.

[*To* POVERTY.] What does it all mean?

POVERTY.

I fear you have been swindled.

MRS. MABY.

[*Overhearing* POVERTY.] Oh, Lord Poverty! My God! 'tis impossible.

POVERTY.

The boy said so, and then became umconscious.

MRS. SMILE.

[*Aside.*] This is what I feared.

MR. MABY.

[*To* TAYLOR.] Where is Sirao?

TAYLOR.

In the lodge.

MR. MABY.

[*To* MRS. MABY.] I'll see him.

MRS. MABY-

Do, do! Learn the truth! Quick or I'll go mad!

MR. MABY.

[*To* MRS. MABY.] This alarm of yours, to

say the least is imprudent. [*To* ALL.] Accept my assurance that Maxey has not told the truth. [*To* MRS. MABY *and* POVERTY.] In the name of all that's prudent, prevent if possible, this scare from spreading beyond the limits of this house. [*To his wife.*] A scandal at this time even before we know the truth! We're not babies, to be frightened at the boo of a half crazed urchin.

MRS. MABY.

But George —

MR. MABY.

Do as I say! Quiet your fears — follow my directions. [*Turning and addressing all.*] Come, join us; we've a plate for all.

MRS. SMILE.

Very kind of you, but —

MR. MABY.

[*To* MRS. SMILE.] No, buts! You must remain, and listen for the guns.

MR. SMILE.

Guns?

MR. MABY.

Yes — fired from Tower hill. One, means victory; two, that we've won by a majority of fifty or more, and three, that our plurality exceeds one hundred.

MRS. SMILE.

[*To her husband.*] We must certainly wait.

HELEN.

I wish they'd fire them now.

MRS. MABY.

[*With a forced laugh.*] Come! It's been a day of anxiety, but our victory will more than compensate us for all.

MR. MABY.

[*To his wife.*] I shall interview Sirao at once.

MRS. MABY.

Do — let me know —

MR. MABY.

[*Interrupting.*] The truth. [*Guests are about retiring. Noise heard in vestibule. Enters* RUSHFOOT *wearing long ulster, with capacious pockets. Left pocket bulging out, and carefully buttoned. Small slouch hat, the left leg of trousers hanging from top of his boot. General appearance indicates anxiety, haste and annoyance. Hangs ulster up after taking it off.*]

RUSHPOOT.

Think of it! On election day! Imagine it! [*To* OLD MABY.] A fox hunt today, or any day.

MR. SMILE.

The sport is inspiring.

RUSHFOOT.

Think of it! Women by the score. men by the hundreds, lackeys by the dozen, all on reckless horse-flesh, preceded by a gang of big fanged, yelping dogs, the whole outfit dashing pell mell, over ditches and hedges in devil-may-care unison, pursiung a little fox. If it was a Mavrick steer, or a long horned Spanish bull, that would be different — but a little fox.

MRS. SMILE.

They follow the hounds in the States.

RUSHFOOT.

Not in my country, except those, who are in the metamorphic state; that is, in the process of transition from vulgar obscurity, to the lower conditions of polite society. [*Enters* TAYLOR. *Hands card on salver to* RUSHFOOT.]

MRS. MABY.

Come! [*Taking* MRS. SMILE *by the arm.*] we'll listen for the guns, [*Guests file out right entrance. Enters* CAPTAIN EMERY.]

RUSHFOOT.

[*To* SALLY, *seen near right entrance,*] Bring me a slice of bread and a glass of water. [SALLY *retires. Reading card.*] "Captain Tilford Emery." [*Sees* EMERY.] Captain Emery, I'm pleased to meet you.

EMERY.

[*Small dapper looking Englishman in uniform. Wears a monocle.*] Thanks awfully. [*Bows.*]

RUSHFOOT.

Will you step into the drawing room?

EMERY.

No, thanks — awfully. But a minute! I'am the bearer of a message from Major Bradford, rather [*Handing* RUSHFOOT *letter.*] a distressing communication, [*Bows.*] but you know a gentleman's honor is at stake.

RUSHFOOT.

[*Opening and running his eye over the letter.*] Whose honor?

EMERY.

Major Bradford's

RUSHFOOT.

[*Reading.*] Poor devil! [*Without lifting his eyes from letter.*]

EMERY.

[*With dignity*.] What do you mean, sir?

RUSHFOOT.

You say the Major's honor is at stake.

EMERY.

Sir — he claims —

RUSHFOOT.

[*To* TAYLOR.] Say to his Lordship, that I wish to see him. [*To* EMERY.] Pardon me, the whole business is here. [*Reads*.] "Sir,"— "You have applied, in a public and shameful manner". [*Listens for the guns*.] Let me see I got as far as the Major's „shameful manner."— [*Reads*.] "You have applied, in a public and shameful manner, by cowardly innuendo, an opprobrious epithet to my name. I am not a mule, neither am I an ass." [*Enters* SALLY *with bread etc.*] Excuse me Captain I havn't had a bite since morning. [*Looks at letter*.] We got to the Major's assertion, that he was not an ass.

[*Reads.*] "But sir a"— What's that word? [*Hands letter to* EMERY.]

EMERY.

[*Adjusting his monocle.*] What word, sir?

RUSHFOOT.

[*Points out the word with a piece of the crust of the bread he has just broken.*] That one.

EMERY.

[*Looking at it.*] "Gentleman." [*Snappishly.*]

RUSHFOOT.

[*Laughing.*] I never should have suspected it. "Gentleman." [*Laughing.*] "And as such, I demand of you a prompt apology for your cowardly insult. Otherwise Captain Emery the bearer of this message, is authorized to act for me in conjunction with any gentleman you may name, to make such arrangements as the satisfaction I demand of you, calls for. I have the honor"— [*Enters* POVERTY.]

EMERY.

[*Bowing.*] I trust your lordship is well.

POVERTY.

Yes — quite, thank you.

RUSHFOOT.

[*Hands* POVERTY *letter.*] I'm called out.

POVERTY.

[*Looking at letter.*] A challenge? Of course. What's the trouble?

RUSHFOOT.

The Major's honor has been thrown out of gear.

POVERTY.

Readjust it. Why not?

EMERY.

I trust your Lordship hasn't inherited the prejudice, your father had, against the code.

RUSHFOOT.

[*To* EMERY.] We don't fight duels in my country. Of course politicians do. Public rejoicing encourages such encounters, because they often prove fatal.

POVERTY.

The *duello* is a rank weed; it's a medieval thing; it's been stamped out long ago.

RUSHFOOT.

[*To* EMERY.] Men of courage don't fight, now.

EMERY.

Very well, my lord, you know the consequences.

RUSHFOOT.

[*To* EMERY.] I don't want to kill your friend.

EMERY.

[*To* POVERTY.] Your principal will be posted in every club—

RUSHFOOT.

[*Interrupting. To* POVERTY.] This medieval

weed, you speak of, grows only in the sloughs of giddy club life. No decent body of gentlemen tolerate the rank growth.

EMERY.

[*To* POVERTY.] I wait your lordship's pleasure. [*Goes toward left entrance.*]

RUSHFOOT.

[*To* EMERY.] Suppose we fight — think of his wife and daughter.

POVERTY.

Of course — it would be a shame to drive them into crape.

RUSHFOOT.

Suppose I get killed — cut off in the youth of my old age — damn it! — crowded off Gods earth — by — [*To himself.*] a red nosed, red headed English Major. [*To* POVERTY.] I'll fight at any time, at any place.

POVERTY.

Why not — I'll stand around with the Captain.

EMERY.

Stand around?

POVERTY.

Of course — while your man and mine are trying to kill each other. Why not? [*Cannon heard without.*]

RUSHFOOT.

Hurrah, George has won! "Maby and Arbitration, forever!"

POVERTY.

[*Confidentially.*] Don't you think your affair with the major, is a subject for arbitration.

RUSHFOOT.

Never! I'll fight and arbitrate the matter with his widow afterwards. [*Enters* HELEN, *followed by guests.*]

HELEN.

[*To* RUSHFOOT.] Papa, didn't you hear a cannon.

RUSHFOOT.

Yes.

HELEN.

Oh! [*To* MRS. MABY.] Brother George has won.

RUSHFOOT.

[*Taking out his watch.*] Hark! [*Second gun is heard.*] By a majority of fifty or more!

OLD MABY.

Where is Hawkins now? [*Enters* TAYLOR.]

TAYLOR.

A message for Mr. Rushfoot.

RUSHFOOT.

[*Taking massage from salver.*] This tells the whole story.

OLD MABY.

[*Listening.*] Hark!

RUSHFOOT.

Two cannon only! George has a majority of fifty six —

MR. SMILE.

By jove, the credit of this victory is due to you, Mr. Rushfoot.

POVERTY.

[*Shaking* RUSHFOOT'S *hand.*] Why not?

MR. SMILE.

[*To* RUSHFOOT.] How you did it I cant say, but you broke the hunt up.

MRS. SMILE.

[*Looking at her husband.*] Fortunately.

MR. SMILE.

Fortunately.

OLD MABY.

[*Who has been talking with* RUSHFOOT.] No! Ha—ha—ha, you did? Ha—ha—ha, that's great! regular cowboy. Its all over; tell it. Ha—ha—ha—

MR. SMILE,

It's evidently a good joke, tell it.

RUSHFOOT,

When I heard of the hunt, I determined to break it up. Mounting "Fleeting John," that one of the stable men was exercising, I located the run, overtook and outstripped the party, hounds and all. Near the old well, I saw the mite of a beast the gang were after. When within twenty feet of him, I swung from my seat in the saddle, and swiped him.

MR. SMILE,

That will do for a joke, Mr. Rushfoot.

RUSHFOOT.

[*Getting his ulster and throwing it over his left arm.*] That's right — sure.

MR. SMILE.

Have you any witnesses? [*Laughing.*]

RUSHFOOT.

[*Taking the fox out of his pocket.*] Only one—

MR. SMILE.

That's the fox — black tail and all.

OLD MABY.

There's Yankee intermeddling for you. It has won the day! [*Enters* MR. MABY.]

MR. MABY.

[*To his wife.*] Maxey has destroyed the original.

MRS. MABY.

Oh! [*Falls.*]

RUSHFOOT.

[*Kneeling, and taking* MRS. MABY *in his arms.*] Poor girl, the excitement of the day has over come her.

END OF THE SECOND ACT.

THE THIRD ACT.

There's an elapse of three days between the second and third acts.

The Scene is the same, as in the second act

MR. MABY.

[*Reading letter.*] To day— [*Reflecting.*] is the eighteenth. [*Shaking his head.*] Too late — too late. [*Enters* OLD MABY *with a number of open letters in his hand.*]

OLD MABY.

[*Excited.*] George! The Slopper has petered out

MR. MABY.

Petered out? More ill luck.

OLD MABY.

Good luck I should say. Got our American mail this morning.

MR. MABY.

Well.

OLD MABY.

The great ore chimney, at the southern end of the Slopper broke off. But say, say, George, they ran into the same vein, in the northern end of the Extension, and on the fourth level, they struck a parallel vein of high grade rock. [*Laughs.*] George, say, where is Gower now?

MR. MABY.

[*Reflecting.*] I thought, Gower had but one thousand shares of Extension?

OLD MABY.

The other thousand belonged to Lizzie, Smile made her sell them, no doubt.

MR. MABY.

I came near saving that wretched spunger from bankruptcy once.

OLD MABY.

The Bank of England couldn't accommodate the business methods of this shiftless coxcomb.

MR. MABY.

His wife is penniless.

OLD MABY.

Yes, the shares she kept are worthless. The thousand she sold are — why, when the news gets out, Extension ought to be worth fifteen pounds!

MR. MABY.

We ought to return her Extensions. [*Looks at letter.*]

OLD MABY.

Do as you please. What do the detectives say?

MR. MABY.

Nothing.

OLD MABY.

Nothing?

MR. MABY.

Nothing that helps us to find the original. [*Scrutinizing a passage in letter.*] His bank account has been located.

OLD MABY.

That's something. Good! Was the ten thousand in tact?

MR. MABY.

Not a shilling touched.

OLD MABY.

How fortunate!

MR. MABY.

That fact, they telegraphed yesterday.

OLD MABY.

Well.

MR. MABY.

I telephoned Bonnard and Banks to attach the money. That they did, as appears by this letter. [*Taking a letter from table.*] Sirao was know to the Trafalger Bank as Jacob Kaufmann.

OLD MABY.

The scoundrel!

MR. MABY.

And a clever one! [*Getting up.*] Read [*Handing him letter.*] this report.

OLD MABY.

[*Refusing letter.*] Give me the substance of it.

MR. MABY.

Sirao met Van Elfin at Rome last winter. He found the Dutchman in straightened circumstances, and bought his "Peace" for four thousand pounds.

OLD MABY.

The villian! and charged you ten.

MR. MABY.

Again in ninety four, at Madrid, he sold a Bartolomeo, but delivered a copy. The fraud being detected, he pleaded that the original had been destroyed by fire. The Spaniard fearing he might lose his money aided Sirao to get from the insurance company, the value of his painting. The original was afterwards sold in Paris. On that occasion he had two copies. One, he palmed off on the Spaniard; the other, he burned, saving bits of charred canvas, to prove the loss of the original.

OLD MABY.

Prosecute the scoundrel!

MR. MABY.

At times, I'm tempted to offer the scoundrel five thousand pounds, if he'll produce the original.

OLD MABY.

George, I would disown you!

MR. MABY.

But think of it;— we'll be the laughing stock of all England.

OLD MABY.

Let them laugh.

MR. MABY.

You're right father. The jig is up. I'll notify Marlborough House, that the celebration is to be indefinately postponed.

OLD MABY.

That's it! act the man. [*Enters* SIRAO, *followed by detective, who stands back toward right entrance. To his son.*] Did you send for this — [*Pointing to* SIRAO.]

MR. MABY.

[*Interrupting.*] Yes. [*To* SIRAO.] Look! [*Pointing to the painting.*]

SIRAO.

Yes, Mr. Maby, the Van Elfin, Mr. Maby — the Van Elfin.

MR. MABY.

Where is the original?

SIRAO.

My heart is not black — Mr. Maby — not black.

MR. MABY.

Answer my question!

SIRAO.

I am an artist, — not a cheat — Mr. Maby, My heart—

MR. MABY.

[*Interrupting.*] Don't persist in your deceptions; they'll avail you nothing. You base dog!

SIRAO.

That's unkind Mr. Maby — you do me injury. There's no profit in denunciation.

MR. MABY.

Do you injury — you wretch!

SIRAO.

Gentlemen — I keep cool — I keep my temper.

MR. MABY.

Think you, that England is without a prison— that her laws permit you to play the swindler with impunity?—?

SIRAO.

See me — Mr. Maby — I'm not excited.

MR. MABY.

You are possessed of a prudent temper Jacob Kaufmann.

SIRAO.

[*Startled.*] "Jacob Kaufmann!" [*Laughs.*] I don't know the gentleman.

MR. MABY.

The chairmann of the Trafalger Bank does.

SIRAO.

[*Alarmed.*] Mr. Maby — listen — Maxey, [*Clutching his hands.*] the devil Maxey —

MR. MABY.

Stop! Abide by your own precept. "There's no profit in denunciation."

SIRAO.

He burned it! [*Wrings his hands and clasps them on his head.*] The great Van Elfin! Maxey destroyed it. My God! the world has lost a canvas, that allured the touch of a master. 'Tis burned! tis gone! My great painting! [*To* DETECTIVE.] 'Twas mine. [*To* MR. MABY,] My heart is not black— Mr. Maby. [*Beckons* MR. MABY *to one side.*] I'll return your money — [*Confidentially.*] the insurance company will pay me. You, and the nice ladies, and the art critic can help me get mine. See my heart — Mr. Maby.

MR. MABY.

[*With disgust.*] Sirao, understand me, I know your methods. You're in England not in Spain.

You'll never swindle an insurance company here, as you did there. Once more — where is the original?

SIRAO.

[*Agitated with conflicting emotions of wrath, and despair.*] You are a dev— damn— [*Grits his theet.*] Oh! Mr. Maby — please Mr. Maby — don't rob me, don't ruin me. My God, don't! What is there I can do, to convince you that I speak the truth. I will go to London with you, I will do anything. You are smart — you have wealth — take care — in refusing to believe me you rob yourself. [*Laughs.*] Time will tell. My God, I speak the truth!

MR. MABY.

[*To* DETECTIVE.] Take him away! Lodge him in jail to-night.

SIRAO.

[*Excited.*] Damn, have a care — [DETECTIVE *approaches to hand-cuff him. Sirao clutches the air and grits his teeth, as the former comes near him.*] Go away, you beast! go away!

Damn, you dog! You beast of a private detective. [DETECTIVE *handcuffs him, after a struggle.*]

MR. MABY.

Take him away!

SIRAO.

[*With resignation.*] You have a care; my solicitor will be here to night. [*At the right entrance.*] My last word — time will tell. Oh God! Mr. Maby, the picture is burned. [MR. MABY *makes a motion to detective to take him away*] Bah! [*To* MR. MABY.] You damn! [*Grits his teeth and spits toward* MR. MABY.] You devil! [*Stamps and spits again.*] Bah! [*Exit with* DETECTIVE.]

OLD MABY.

[*Shaking his head.*] I fear—

MR. MABY.

What?

OLD MABY.

That his lying throat utters the truth.

MR. MABY.

That Maxey has burned the original?

OLD MABY.

Yes.

MR. MABY.

What motive could the boy have had?

OLD MABY.

Revenge — goaded into madness by abuse. Say — say, didn't he snatch a painting from our new girl, and destroy it in the presence of Mrs. Smile? The girl says so.

MR. MABY.

Did Emma send for Lizzie?

OLD MABY.

Yes.

MR. MABY.

When?

OLD MABY.

After breakfast. [*Looking at his watch.*] 'Tis

one now. Strange! 'Tis worth one's life to venture out in this fog.

MR. MABY.

Well — [*Going toward left entrance.*] MARLBOROUGH HOUSE must be notified. [*Exit* MR. MABY.]

OLD MABY.

[*Rings.*] The devil take the whole business! [*Enters* TAYLOR.]

TAYLOR.

Yes, sir? [*Bowing.*]

OLD MABY.

Brandy! [*Exit* TAYLOR *at right entrance, bowing. Enters* RUSHFOOT *left entrance, heavy overcoat on and looking generally dilapidated.*]

RUSHFOOT.

[*Turning his coat collar down.*] Say Maby— why in the devil don't your race move? Your old island is enveloped, more than half the time, in a black mist, as dense as the expulsions of a smoke-stack. [*Enters* TAYLOR *with brandy.*]

OLD MABY.

You growl at our chimate, but never at our brandy. [*Laughs.*]

RUSHFOOT.

The blessed stuff — never! [OLD MABY *fills two glases.*] Your health! [*Drinks.*] Thats good. Brandy is a trouble hunter — it's reaching. Nothing on earth dispels the gloom of a man's soul [*Fills his glass.*] quicker than a glass — [*Drinks.*] than two glasses of good brandy.

OLD MABY.

Devilish weather!

RUSHFOOT.

The fog is so thick, that I'll bet the Queen hasn't found her throne to day, unless some one slept on it all night, and gave the old lady a toot on a horn this morning.

OLD MABY.

The fog or the Queen doesn't concern me, but the Prince of Wales does,

RUSHFOOT.

Has he been notified?

OLD MABY.

A messenger leaves for London this afternoon. George must not delay the matter another moment. [*Goes toward left entrance.*] Such beastly luck! [*Exit. Enters* JACK.]

JACK.

[*Goes up to* RUSHFOOT, *and grasps him warmly by the hand.*] I'm so glad to see you.

RKSHFOOT.

Evidently.

JACK.

[*Looking him over.*] Not a scratch, good! Did you pepper him?

RUSHFOOT.

Who?

JACK.

The Britisher.

RUSHFOOT.

[*Hesitatingly.*] N—o.

JACK.

Too bad.

RUSHFOOT.

Who told you.

JACK.

[*Puts his fingers to his lips.*] I knew all about it.

RUSHFOOT.

[*Looks at* JACK *and smiles. Helen appears at right entrance.*] Have a drink!

JACK.

Certainly! [HELEN *alarmed.*]

Are you much of a drinker? [*Pouring out brandy for* JACK.]

JACK.

I can hold my own.

RUSHFOOT.

[*Still pouring.*] Say when.

JACK.

A little more!

RUSHFOOT.

[*Still pouring.*] How's that?

JACK.

Just a little more. [RUSHFOOT *continuing.*] There, there — thanks.

RUSHFOOT.

Your health!

JACK.

[*Touching glasses.*] Pardon my curiosity, but [*Drinks.*] did you — [*Coughs violently.*] meet [*Coughs.*] Major Brad — [*Coughs.*] ford?

RUSHFOOT.

[*Laughs.*] You do hold your own, just about.

JACK.

[*With handkerchief to his eyes.*] Did you say— you met him?

RUSHFOOT.

No, we got lost in the fog.

JACK.

Too bad. I leave for America to-night. I cannot go without informing you, that the London press have been asked to investigate the Sirao swindle, and have sent men here for that purpose.

RUSHFOOT.

[*To himself.*] Poor Emma! [*To* JACK.] We want to keep the affair out of the press.

JACK.

Some one here, no doubt, a woman sent an anonymous letter to the London dailies, alleging that the gift of a copy of Van Elfin's Peace, and the intended ceremonies, incident to its presentation to the Arbitration League, were the devices of a Yankee woman, conceived for the sole purpose, of gaining social notoriety. That an exposure of the plot, will, no doubt, save the Prince of Wales from being inveigled into the scheme of honoring the occasion by his royal presence, and so forth, and so forth.

RUSHFOOT.

This is monstrous! Human malevolence has some limitations! You have been deceived, this story can't be true.

JACK.

I saw the letter. A reporter believing me to be here, as the Earth representative, on the same mission as himself, gave me the letter to copy.

RUSHFOOT.

Can you get the letter again.

JACK.

I havn't copied it yet, it's in my room.

RUSHFOOT.

Get it, quick! Show it to Mr. George Maby!

JACK.

[*Going toward left entrance.*] There is no impropriety in that. It's only a devil's pigeon.

RUSHFOOT.

Devil's pigeon? What's that?

JACK.

An anonymous letter. [*Exit* JACK.]

RUSHFOOT.

"Devil's pigeon." [*Helping himself to another glass.*] The devil's pigeon — the foul hatch of a foul heart. [*Drinks.*] Life has its compensations. [*Enters* POVERTY, *hat pulled down; coat turned up, and carries pistol case.* RUSHFOOT *takes* POVERTY *by the hand. With dignity.*] My lord, how did you lose me?

POVERTY.

[*Surprised.*] Lose you?

RUSHFOOT.

Yes, my lord.

POVERTY.

Of course, to be sure — why not? You got out of the carriage, and didn't come in again.

RUSHFOOT.

[*Smiling and putting his hand on* POVERTY'S *shoulder. Shows slight effect of the brandy.*] Listen, listen my boy! After getting out of the carriage, I — I looked about to see where we were. The fog was so thick, that I couldn't find the thing again. The real fact was this. [*Laughs.*] Poverty — my dear Pov— [*Laughing.*] I forgot which end of our carriage, the horses were on. [*Laughing.*] Have a drink.

POVERTY.

Why not? [*They drink.*]

RUSHFOOT.

I'm sorry. I wouldn't have disappointed the major for one hundred thousand dollars.

POVERTY.

Of course not. But you see, I fixed it.

RUSHFOOT.

[*Surprised.*] How?

POVERTY.

After the doctor and I, the driver, the horses and carriage lost you—

RUSHFOOT.

[*Laughs.*] That's good.

POVERTY.

We knocked about for a bit, making Rams Knoll, after two hours of fine swearing. On the way we ran into Bradford's party, lost in a bank of fog, so thick that a bird couldn't flutter through it. I jawed Emery, and asked him, why he hadn't met us. He replied, with some sort of foggy apologies, and then made a rush for the carriage to gab more, when he fell into a ditch. While they were hauling him out we moved on.

RUSHFOOT.

[*Offering* POVERTY *his hand.*] Shake my boy,

shake! That's right. [*They shake hands.*] When you fabricate do it with arrant grandeur. Now for one more! [RUSHFOOT *fills glasses.*]

POVERTY.

Your health, why not?

RUSHFOOT.

[*Laughing.*] You did indeed fool the whole Bradford outfit. [*Holding up glass.*] As they say in Cripple Creek, here's that your life may be crowded with extravagant satisfactions and high grade indulgences.

POVERTY.

[*Holding up glass.*] Here's that the Major will miss you.

RUSHFOOT.

And that I'll hit him— [*They drink.*] weather permitting.

POVERTY

Of course. But he may apologize.

RUSHFOOT.

He ought to, he knows now that I wasn't thrown.

POVERTY.

Yes, but the Major said you called him an ass. He says that if you apologize, he will. Meet him half way, why not?

RUSHFOOT.

My lord don't — I'm sensitive — don't — because I like you. You don't run much to sentiment, but brains are in your head.

POVERTY.

I think so — I'm not sure.

RUSHFOOT.

Apologize — never!

POVERTY.

Then it's fight?

RUSHFOOT.

Sure. I'll teach the Major that to challenge

an American is a damned serious affair. [*Enters* TAYLOR.]

TAYLOR.

[*To* RUSHFOOT.] Your lunch, sir.

RUSHFOOT.

Have you a plate for his lordship?

TAYLOR.

Yes sir. [*Bows and retires.*]

RUSHFOOT.

[*Going toward right entrance.*] Come.

POVERTY.

Why not?

RUSHFOOT.

Apologize, no!

POVERTY.

Of course — Why not? [*Exeunt* RUSHFOOT *and* POVERTY. *Bell rings. Enters* JACK, *followed by* SALLY.]

JACK.

[*Taking letter from his pocket.*] Give this to Mr. George Maby.

SALLY.

Yes sir. [*Retires.*]

JACK.

[*Musing.*] Things are twisted in this house. [*Enters* HELEN.] My own affairs are not entirely straight.

HELEN.

[*Approaching* JACK *and putting her arm around him.*] What are you thinking of, Jack?

JACK.

[*Looking at* HELEN *sternly.*] Of a fool.

HELEN.

[*Seriously,*] There is one in this house.

JACK.

Very likely.

HELEN.

[*Looking at* JACK *very tenderly.*] Jack, did the picture suggest the idea?

JACK.

[*To himself.*] "Her last dupe"— [*To* HELEN.] It suggested nothing, it told me everything.

HELEN.

[*Looking.*] Yes, I'm so sorry, but what's done can't be undone.

JACK.

[*To himself.*] Isn't this refreshing? [*To* HELEN.] You're unkind, to put it mildly.

HELEN.

I may be — 'tis not sisterly.

JACK.

Sisterly!

HELEN.

No. [*Quietly.*] Jack, I've talked the matter over with papa.

JACK.

Well — what does he say?

HELEN.

He says there are three kinds of cheek. There's cheek, brass, and sublime confidence.

JACK.

[*Looking at* HELEN *sternly.*] Seeking you beneath this roof, was no doubt a piece of cheek.

HELEN.

Yes, but it was so good of you, Jack.

JACK.

Posing as an art critic was another —

HELEN.

Yes a piece of effulgent, heroic effrontery. It was grand! [*Laughing.*]

JACK.

[*Taking his hat.*] I'm off to America.

HELEN.

Jack!

JACK.

[*Goes to left entrance.*] Before going permit me to say, that when a girl forces a fellow, whom she pretends to love, into another room, in order to make love, to one she doesn't profess to love, possesses a transcendental nerve, shoved clear through the roof of the superlative degree. "Your last dupe." [*Exit* JACK.]

HELEN.

[*Following* JACK.] Jack! Come back! I love you. [*Enters* BENSON.] Oh Heavens! [*To herself.*] What a mess! What does Jack mean? [BENSON *approaches* HELEN.] Oh, Miss Benson! [BENSON *hands* HELEN *a letter.* HELEN *opens it and starts to read.*] Oh dear, this is not for me!

BENSON.

His lordship. [*Bowing.* HELEN *returns letter.*]

HELEN.

[*To herself.*] I don't know what I'm doing. What does Jack mean? [*To* BENSON.] Lord Poverty is lunching with papa. [BENSON *bows and goes in drawing room. Enters* EFFIE.]

EFFIE.

Why, Mr. Randolph is returning to America isnt he?

HELEN.

[*In despair.*] Oh, did you see him?

EFFIE.

Yes, just as I entered, he bade me good bye. Dear! he was awfully excited!

HELEN.

[*In undertone, looking toward drawing room, and then at Effie. The latter understands Helen's glance and answers in like manner.*] Effie pity me — pity me! [*Puts handkerchief to her eyes.*] I am forsaken.

EFFIE.

Forsaken?

HELEN.

[*Nods.*] Yes — forsaken.

EFFIE.

[*Consoling her.*] What is the matter?

HELEN.

[*Reflecting.*] Do you know Lord Poverty well? [*Tragically,*] Has he got a memory? Is his promise to be relied on?

EFFIE.

[*Surprised.*] Why yes.

HELEN.

[*To herself.*] I see it all. [*To* EFFIE.] You are deceived. [*To herself.*] He has forgotten to tell Jack, that I was to help him hoodwink this old creature here. [*Nodding her head toward* BENSON.] Oh! [*Walking up and down the stage.*] Self preservation is the first law of nature. [*Looks at* EFFIE *and then at* BENSON. *To* EFFIE.] I feel like a lioness that's lost her only whelp, that's lost her only Jack. Oh dear, my head is not on my body, I'm mad!

EFFIE.

Why Helen!

HELEN.

O—h. [*Advancing toward* BENSON, *who appears at entrance of drawing room*, *To* BENSON *in tragic tone.*] Miss Benson, [*Enters* POVERTY.] Lord Poverty doesn't care the snap of his finger for me, and I don't care the snap of my finger for — [*Sees* POVERTY.] for Lord Poverty. [*Falls on sofa*]

POVERTY.

Of course.

BENSON.

[*Approaches* POVERTY.] Your lordship. [*Hands him letter. Bows and retires.*]

HELEN.

[*Jumping up.*] I'm mad.

POVERTY.

Mad, of course.

HELEN.

You are the cause of it. Your love for me was all pretence.

POVERTY.

To be sure — quite right.

EFFIE.

[*Surprised. To* POVERTY.] Is it possible?

POVERTY.

Why not? Only duplicity. [*Enters* SALLY.]

SALLY.

[*To* HELEN.] Madame wants to see you himmediately, Miss Helen. [SALLY *retires.*]

HELEN.

[*Going toward left entrance.*] I am lost! [*Exit* HELEN.]

POVERTY.

[*Looking at* EFFIE.] Is the situation clear to you?

EFFIE.

Yes. [*Sighing.*]

POVERTY.

Is it now? — Fancy!

EFFIE.

Quite clear.

POVERTY.

What is the muss?

EFFIE.

[*Slowly.*] Have you ever pretended to love Miss Helen?

POVERTY.

Of course — to be sure.

EFFIE.

And you didn't?

POVERTY.

How could I love her and you at the same time?

EFFIE.

I am sorry to hear this from your own lips, my lord.

POVERTY.

I've been making an ass of myself. I think— I'm not sure. You see, I've been after money.

EFFIE.

Oh Lord Poverty!

POVERTY.

Why not — I might as well have it as anyone else. [*Takes out letter.*] Would you mind if I took a look at this. [*Goes to right of stage and reads and comments to himself.*] Here she raises the devil — [*Turns over page.*] here he's continued. A lecture on economy — her self respect and the pride of the Povertys. Here's the milk of the cocoanut. [*Reads.*] "In view of all I have said, you can't but see the justice of my act — you inherit nothing — my estate is left to the first male issue of your body. Lady Hamilton." The first male issue. 'Twould be a joke if it was a girl. [*Reflects.*] Another girl, another joke. Fine assets. An aunt of mine had thirteen girls I think, I'm not sure. [*To* EFFIE.] You see I've been check-mated. Let her keep her money — the baby will have it. Let me tell you the whole thing.

EFFIE.

[*Alarmed going to left entrance.*] I must go!

POVERTY.

I want a chat with you about the matter.

EFFIE.

I must go, Lord Poverty! [*Enters* OLD MABY, *excited.*]

OLD MABY.

[*To* POVERTY.] Maxey has regained consciousness. He's jabbering away in Italian. Come hurry!

POVERTY.

[*To* EFFIE.] I must talk to you. [*Exeunt* POVERTY *and* OLD MABY.]

EFFIE.

The situation isn't so clear to me now. [*Reflecting*.] I don't dare to think. Oh dear! I have almost loved — I'm frightened, I must go. Pretended to love Helen. [*Enters* JACK. *Doesn't see* EFFIE.]

JACK.

I must at least pay my respects to Old Mr. Maby. Then I'll bid farewell to this infernal place. "Her last dupe." Oh! pretending to love me, when she loved Lord Poverty. [EFFIE *surprised, coughs to attract* JACK'S *attention.*] Miss Revere! Did you get on to — I mean, did you overhear any of my remarks?

EFFIE.

I'm afraid, I did.

JACK.

I thought I was alone.

EFFIE.

Pardon me, but I'm so excited.

JACK.

[*Aside.*] She's tumbled. [*To* EFFIE.] Miss Revere, you are an American, so am I — you're in trouble, so am I — I know it. I've been aped on and so have you.

EFFIE.

Aped on?

JACK.

Yes — monkeyed with — made a fool of. Lord Poverty has pretended to love you, hasn't he.

EFFIE.

Assume he has.

JACK.

[*Confidentially.*] He cares no more for you, than Helen Rushfoot does for me. He's a deceiver, and Helen Rushfoot is — well—

EFFIE.

[*Interrupting.*] I'm horrified! — It can't be true!

JACK.

Do you know the situation? Yet, I have loved that girl.

EFFIE.

[*Faintly.*] Let me get out into the open air.

JACK.

[*To* EFFIE.] My soul is stirred with such — [*To himself.*] damnable emotions — I'll jump the game now. A note will do. [*Aside,*] "Her last dupe." [*Exeunt* EFFIE *and* JACK. *Enters* MR. MABY *from right entrance. He stands as though waiting for some one to follow him. Looks at letter he holds in his hand.]*

MR. MABY.

Astounding! [*Enters* OLD MABY *excited.*]

OLD MABY.

What does Emma say?

MR. MABY.

Nothing.

OLD MABY.

Nothing?

MR. MABY.

She looked at the letter, and recognizing the handwriting of Lizzie Smile, she recoiled at the sight of her friends treachery. I must go. Maxey relapsed, didn't he?

OLD MABY.

Yes, before his lordship reached the chamber.

MR. MABY.

I am going to the hotel to see Mr. Randolph. Something must be done to avert a newspaper scandal. You had better go down to the stable and see how Rushfoot gets on with Sirao.

OLD MABY.

I'll go right away. [*Exit* OLD MABY, *right entrance.*]

MR. MABY.

[*Putting on his hat.*] There are crimes that human speech refuses to describe. This womans act must remain undefined. [*Exit, left entrance.* TAYLOR *appears at right entrance.*]

TAYLOR.

Sally, Sally! Come 'ere! [SALLY *appears.*]

SALLY.

What's hup Bob.

TAYLOR.

There's 'igh jinks hagoing hon hat the stable.

SALLY.

'Igh jinks?

TAYLOR.

Aye. Mr. Rushfoot his trying to force the Hitalian to tell where the pinting his.

SALLY.

Hit's burned — Hi tell you — [*Listens.*] 'Ark, hit's a carriage!

TAYLOR.

Get hout hof 'ere! [*They cross the stage to left entrance and retire. Enters* MRS. SMILE.]

MRS. SMILE.

[*Looks about her.*] Foggy. [*Looks at pictures, taking a position, that commands view of both entrances.*] The shock should have come after and not before their celebration. Well. [*Approaches painting. Examines it with lorgnettes.*] Fate still scowls. [*Taking position as before.*] The pin I stuck in the copy, wouldn't be found in the original. [*Laughs.*] I wonder, if the reporters have been here yet? Emma Maby will find perchance, that a fearless press, knows how to burn and blister the hearts of even the audacious. Think of these Yankee millionaires; they come among us, pamper either to our vanities or prejudices — throw their money here, and elsewhere, as a butcher shys a bone to a gang of scurvey curs, and fancy forsooth, that the gates of royalty, should be thrown open to them. Oh! this sensitive friend of mine. She may yet learn that the road that leads upwards, from the planes of social mediocraty, to the summit of royal favor, is beset with perils. [*Enters* MRS. MABY, *very feeble, grasping objects as she advances* MRS. SMILE *starts to go toward her, but an indefinable gesture from* MRS. MABY, *causes her to forbear.*]

MRS. SMILE.

I am sorry Emma to find you so ill.

MRS. MABY.

Only a nervous spell.

MRS. SMILE.

Anxiety, poor girl.

MRS. MABY.

[*Approaching the picture. Gazes at it while supporting herself by grasping a chair.*] How beautiful! [*Putting her handkerchief to her eyes and silently weeping.*] Come! [*Extending her hand backward without moving her body.*] Come! [*Pulls her hand back as though horrified at her act.* MRS. SMILE *not seeing her extended hand remains motionless.*] Beyond the river, [*Weeps.*] amid the flowers — two maidens walk hand in hand — the taller one looks like — [*Turns and gazes at* MRS. SMILE.] How beautiful you were! [*Weeps.*] And oh, how I loved you! [*Turns again to the painting.*]

MRS. SMILE.

[*To herself.*] Does she suspect? Impossible!

MRS. MABY.

The smaller one — how trustingly she gazes into the eyes of her fair companion. [*Weeps.*]

MRS. SMILE.

Why Emma! you're almost in a state of collapse.

MRS. MABY.

Not now — these tears strengthen me. [*Stands without support.*]

MRS. SMILE.

Emma, you are too ambitious.

MRS. MABY.

[*Looking at her handkerchief, that she twists, nervously in her hand.*] No — no, I'm only unhappy.

MRS. SMILE.

You ought to be happy.

MRS. MABY.

[*Looking at* MRS. SMILE.] Ought to be happy? [*Greatly moved.*]

MRS. SMILE.

In your present nervous condition, you'll be unequal to the task of entertaining royalty.

MRS. MABY.

[*With spirit.*] The higher type of my country

women require no nerve, nothing but heart, to entertain a Prince, without it they couldn't entertain a pauper.

MRS. SMILE.

[*Sarcastically.*] English women esteem it a high privilege to act the hostess to a guest, as exalted as his Royal Highness. You Americans may regard such presence, as a mere incident to a generous spread — giving the matter no farther thought, than that, of telling the butler to drop an extra plate on the table.

MRS. MABY.

[*With spirit.*] I am the wife of a British subject. My husbands solicitude for the comfort of a guest should be shared by me, but let me assure you, that beneath this roof, royalty possessing the true qualities of gentility, will find the fullest measure of honest cheer. The presence of His Highness at my "generous spread", will not be signalized by the dropping of an extra plate on my table — nor shall I, a descendant of one who expired at Bunker Hill drop my self respect, as I would drop an old garment, to cringe, stammer and scrape, in the presence of any human creature, prince, king or potentate.

MRS. SMILE.

As the wife of a British subject, you'll discover that the homage due to His Highness is prescribed by inexorable canons, the infraction of which may, to say the least, render yon open to the common criticism, that—

MRS. MABY.

That what?

MRS. SMILE.

"That court obeisance, gauls only"—

MRS. MABY.

Yes?

MRS. SMILE.

"The republican parvenu."

MRS. MABY.

[*Indignantly.*] Epigrammatic slander has no

terrors for me. If facts justify these detestible words, then the great republic is a lie — a patchwork of illusions and silly dreams. Let me deal in honest words, words that have not been whipped into a smart phrase, to humiliate the groveling sycophant of royalty, but words that proclaim the nobility of a race, which dwells beyond the seas, and those words are, madame that within the sovereignties of the Great Republic, we kneel to none, but God, and our mothers.

MRS SMILE.

Why Emma! I marvel at the sublimity of your spirit. After all you can't blame one for sticking up for one's own country. Perhaps I made a mistake, in presuming upon the friendship of years to hint, that after all, social ambition is but the heart burn of wealth.

MRS. MABY.

Socially, I ask nothing, but what belongs to me. What you are pleased to call my social aims, I call my social rights. [*Falls into a chair.*]

I sent for you, this morning to ask you about — but it doesn't matter, and in fact, I regret — that — you came. [*To herself.*] I can't accuse her. [*Enters* HELEN, *excited.*]

HELEN.

[*Excited.*] Maxey —! [*Surprised at seeing* MRS. SMILE.]

MRS. SMILE.

Emma, can I do anything for you.

MRS. MABY.

[*Without looking at her.*] Yes, step into the drawing room.

MRS. SMILE.

[*Looks at* HELEN *then at* MRS. MABY.] Certainly. [*Goes to drawing room entrance. To Aside.*] Strange, very strange! [*Retires.*]

HELEN.

Maxey has regained consciousness!

MRS. MABY.

Who's with him?

HELEN.

Lord Poverty.

MRS. MABY.

Has he spoken?

HELEN.

Not yet. He sat up in bed, looked about and then fell back and began to cry.

MRS. MABY.

[*Going toward left entrance.*] Poor boy. [*Retires.*]

HELEN.

[*Looking toward drawing room door.*] Madame Treachery, I hope never to see your face again. [*Exit* HELEN. *Enter* RUSHFOOT *and* OLD MABY.]

RUSHFOOT.

It's destroyed.

OLD MABY.

George insists, that Sirao is playing his Spanish trick on us.

RUSHFOOT.

He's wrong; Sirao could no more deliver to him Van Elfin's Peace, than an assassin could call from the grave, the victim of his treachery.

OLD MABY.

I's no use. [*Enters* MR. MABY.]

MR. MABY.

[*Excited.*] The reporters insist upon seeing the painting; they're coming over directly. There must be no excitement. I've admitted nothing; said nothing. [*To* RUSHFOOT.] Did you get anything out of Sirao?

RUSHFOOT.

Enough to convince me, that he's telling the truth. I've turned him over to a police constable.

OLD MABY.

Charged with attempt to murder.

MR. MABY.

Not with swindling?

OLD MABY.

No— you'll have plenty of time to lodge that complaint against him later on.

MR. MABY.

You're right. 'Twould only add fuel to the fire. [*Enter* MRS. MABY *and* HELEN, *excited.*]

MRS. MABY.

Maxey is up!

MR. MABY.

Up?

MRS. MABY.

Yes, and dressed. Taylor is taking him down.

RUSHFOOT.

What does he say?

MRS. MABY.

He's half delirious.

MR. MABY.

Did he say anything about the painting?

MRS. MABY.

Nothing intelligible.

HELEN.

[*Who has been watching.*] Here he comes. [*Enters* MAXEY, *pale and weak. His head is bandaged and a silk shawl is trown over his shoulders. He is supported by* TAYLOR, *who walks behind him. He jabbers to* POVERTY, *who has entered with him in* ITALIAN, *and then in broken* ENGLISH.]

MAXEY.

Dove mi porti? (*Where are you taking me*)?

POVERTY.

Dove ti porto? Dia tuoi amici. ["*Where am I taking you*". *Among your friends.*]

MAXEY.

Mi porti da mia sorella in Italia. (Take me to my sister in Italy.)

POVERTY.

Take you to your sister. Of course — we'll send you to her. (Da tua sorella? Dicerto, ti manderemo da lei.)

MAXEY.

[*Sinks to the floor.*] Mamma mia! (Mother!) [*Cries.*]

POVERTY.

[*To* MRS. MABY.] The lad calls for his dead mother. He's hardly conscious. [MRS. MABY *weeps.*]

MAXEY.

[*Starts. Looks about him; sees the painting In terror.*] Mi amazzera! Ainto auto! (He will kill me! Hide me!) [*Trys to stand.*]

POVERTY.

Sirao, won't kill you; we wont let him. You

needn't hide. (Sirao, non ti amazzera, non c'e bis agno di ainto.)

MAXEY.

[*Looks at* POVERTY *scrutinizing his face.*] No, Lei non e'. (No—o. You're not—)?

POVERTY.

No. I'm not Sirao. (No, non sono Sirao.)

MAXEY.

[*Sees* MRS. MABY.] Lada! lada! [*Points to picture.*] Origa! origa!

RUSHFOOT.

He says this in the original.

MR. MABY.

[*Points to painting.*] This? [*Goes up to painting and puts his finger on it.*] This? [*Nods.*] This?

MAXEY.

[*Shakes his head.*] Bada! bada! [*Points again to painting.*] Origa!

RUSHFOOT.

First he says it's the original, and then he says it isn't.

POVERTY.

[*Talks to* MAXEY, *who has become very weak, but rational. All gather about to hear the outcome. To* RUSHFOOT.] The thing is all right. [POVERTY *looks toward painting.*] Of course—why not? [*Speaks a few hurried words to* RUSHFOOT *and then to* MR. MABY.]

RUSHFOOT.

[*Hastily examines back end of frame.*] That's right! [*To* POVERTY.] Sure!

MR. MABY.

[*Exited, pulls out his watch.*] The train leaves in twenty minutes! [*To* TAYLOR.] Rush to the stable!— tell Harry to mount, and ride for his life to the station, have Phillips return to Devon House at once. Quick! Not a moment to lose!

TAYLOR.

Yes sir. [*Retires in haste.* SALLY *from left entrance.*]

SALLY.

[*To* MR. MABY.] Three gentlemen from the 'otel his hacoming hup the front driveway sir.

MR. MABY.

The reporters! [*To his father.*] Take Maxey into the drawing room, quick!

OLD MABY.

[*Taking* MAXEY *in his arms.*] Come, my boy, you're among friends [*Exit carrying* MAXEY. *Enters Sirao, handcuffed to* POLICE CONSTABLE, *at right entrance.*]

POLICE CONSTABLE.

[*To* MR. MABY.] The prisoner wants a word with you, sir. [*Enters* SALLY, *followed by reporters.*]

SALLY.

[*To* MR. MABY.] The gentlemen want to see Mr. Maby, sir. [SALLY *retires.*]

MR. MABY.

[*To* POVERTY.] This stupid constable! Get

them both out! Don't allow the handcuffs to be seen! [*To* REPORTERS.] Gentlemen, I am pleased to meet you again.

POVERTY.

[*Taking newspaper from the table. Takes Sirao and constable by manacled arms from behind, throws paper in front of him, so as to conceal handcuffs. Whispers to* SIRAO *and officer. To* MR. MABY.] Just a moment. [*All three bow.*] Just a moment. [*They continue to bow, as they back toward right entrance.*] Why not? [*Exeunt.*]

REPORTER.

If you will pardon us, Mr. Maby, we failed to gather from our last interview with you, at the hotel, whether you were in possession of Van Elfins master piece or only a copy.

MR. MABY.

[*Pointing to* PAINTING.] There, gentlemen, is the copy. [*Enters* POVERTY.]

POVERTY.

[*To* REPORTERS.] Of course.

RUSHFOOT.

[*Drawing out copy from the end of frame.* And here gentlemen, is the original! [*The colors of original are brighter. The illumination of painting, by turning on gas of all the jets at the same instant, is greater.*]

POVERTY.

To be sure.

MR. MABY.

Just a little surprise to entertain our friends. [*Looking at* MRS. SMILE.]

POVERTY.

Why not?

MRS. SMILE.

A surprise indeed. [*Laughing long and loud.*]

THE END OF THE THIRD ACT.

THE FOURTH ACT.

There's an elapse of three days between the third and fourth acts.

The SCENE is the large drawing room in POVERTY CASTLE, five miles from DORCHESTER OAKS. Facing the audience, is an arched entrance, with pillars on each side, leading into large hall. On the left of stage, is an entrance leading into the modern wing of castle, and on right, another entrance to the deserted quarters. The room is a cheerless one. The walls are decorated, with portraits of women in court trains, knights in armor, hunting scenes, etc. etc. Ancient armor, swords and battle axes are distributed about the room. The portraits, on the wall, are hung in an irregular manner, tilted to right and left. Large ancient table stands in centre of room, with chairs, strewed about, without pretense to order. The appearance of the room suggests dust and cobwebs. POVERTY *is discovered, examining papers, that he takes from an old chest on the table.*

POVERTY.

Me assets are low. [*Takes another paper from box.*] God don't think much of money, or He'd [*Looks in box.*] give more of it to his best chaps. [*Looking for another paper.*] Now and then, a decent man has millions [*Examining box.*] dumped on him. [*Looking at audience.*] Too much of the stuff is awkward, they tell me. You can't chuck junks of it, at the howl of every beggar, neither can you bag it all; without being called an ass in the first instance, and a hog in the second. This was the wise observation of an American millionaire, and a fine chap he was — they tell me. Personally, I rather be a [*Examining box.*] hog, and wallow in the dough, than an [*Examining box.*] ass, and eat the thistles of envious criticism.

[*Throws papers in box, and crams them down.*] It's not there. [*Pulls bell cord. Cracked bell rings with a noisy ding.*] Where can it be? [*Enters* BULLOCK — *a fat, beefy looking servant, with a cockney accent.*] Bullock — where are me other assets?

BULLOCK.

Hin the Harches Tower, me lud.

POVERTY.

Bring them here — take these out.

BULLOCK.

Himmediately me lud. [*Places box on floor. Puts documents, that have fallen on the table into box, and stamps on them.*]

POVERTY.

[*Watching him.*] Thats right, Bullock — be careful — don't lose any.

BULLOCK.

Pardon the observation, me lud. Hi've never

lost ha paper since Hi've 'ad charge hof the family harchives.

POVERTY.

You're careful, Bullock. Of course.

BULLOCK.

Hi 'opes Hi ham, me lud. [*Takes box up, starts to go, then hesitates.*] Hif your ludship pleases, you've forbidden me to henter the Harches Tower, on haccount of the setting 'en.

POVERTY.

Do you mean, Nancy?

BULLOCK.

No me lud. Nancy 'as 'er nest hin the mahogany wardrobe hof the state chamber. Tis Queen Moll, that's hin the Harches Tower.

POVERTY.

Fancy? I thought it was Nancy. Don't bother about Queen Moll, she's not game.

BULLOCK.

Very well, me lud. [*Starts to go.*]

POVERTY.

Bullock, keep the cat out of the of the state chamber.

BULLOCK.

Hi 'aven't seen the cat, me lud, for some days. [*Starts again.*]

POVERTY.

Bullock!

BULLOCK.

Yes, me lud.

POVERTY.

Get another cat — the rats must be kept down.

BULLOCK.

Himmediately, me lud. [*Exit with box. Enters* HELEN *from right entrance.*]

HELEN.

Why don't Jack come;

POVERTY.

[*Examining papers, he takes from drawer.*] He'll be here. Why not?

HELEN.

[*Seriously.*] I've done something you'll like.

POVERTY.

Of course —

HELEN.

[*Looking at* POVERTY.] Effie is coming here today.

POVERTY.

Is she now!

HELEN.

'Twas good of you, to intercept Jack at Liverpool for me.

POVERTY.

To be sure. You see he registered at the Adelphi. Finding him out, I dropped him a line, saying that we were all going to America, on the next steamer, and asking him to return to Dorchester Oaks, and go with us.

HELEN.

What did Jack say in his answer? Please tell me every word.

POVERTY.

He said he thought, you were trying to pull my [*Looks in drawer.*] hand for a title.

HELEN.

[*With surpressed laugh, but with mock seriousness.*] Are you sure, he said hand.

POVERTY.

[*Looking at* HELEN.] I think so — I'm not sure. And he said he was sorry to hear, that you were [*Looking at paper.*] dying.

HELEN.

Dying?

POVERTY

Yes — dying on account of him.

HELEN.

Lord Poverty! you didn't write him any such stuff, as that, did you?

POVERTY.

I told him, that you were mushed on him.

HELEN.

Oh! Don't, don't! [*Wringing her hands and laughing.*] It isn't mushed, it's m-a-s-h-e-d, mashed!

POVERTY.

Yes— why not?— of course. But you see it's too late now, I wrote it m-u-s-h-e-d,— mushed. It's quite the same — why not?

HELEN.

Oh dear me! All this humiliation, all this sorrow, comes from the awful mistake you made, Lord Poverty.

POVERTY.

Of course — I quite see that.

HELEN.

Jack is so jealous.

POVERTY.

Jealous, why not?

HELEN.

If Jack had known, that it was only a game to deceive Benson, he would have enjoyed it so — so much.

POVERTY.

So much? Of course.

HELEN.

Oh, I wish Jack would come! [*Seriously*.] Do you know, I've been all over your castle.

POVERTY.

Have you, now?

HELEN.

Lord Poverty — your roof leaks.

POVERTY.

Does it?

HELEN.

Yes, everywhere, except that end. There is no roof on that end. [*Pointing.*] Why don't you stop the leaks at this end? [*Pointing.*]

POVERTY.

You see, the Povertys have always had a weakness for ventilation.

HELEN.

[*Touching table, and then wiping dust off her finger with handkerchief.*] Is your house-keeper a very competent woman?

POVERTY.

The last one was — I've none now.

HELEN.

Has she been gone long?

POVERTY.

Five years, I think.

HELEN.

[*Aside.*] So do I. [*Looking about and shuddering.*] Lord Poverty, you wont be offended, if I ask you a question — will you?

POVERTY.

Nonsense!

HELEN.

You wont think me ill bed.

POVERTY.

Not at all — go on.

HELEN.

If you should ever marry Effie, would you take her, to live here.

POVERTY.

Of course — why not? I'd live in a garret with Maloney — if it leaked. You know, I must have ventilation.

HELEN.

Where would you keep your hens then?

POVERTY.

In the banqueting hall — I think — I'm not sure.

HELEN.

[*Looking at portraits.*] Who were these? [*Pointing to knights.*]

POVERTY.

Povertys.

HELEN.

And the ladies?

POVERPY.

More Povertys.

HELEN.

[*Pointing to portrait.*] Don't you think, that knight is a little skewed.

POVERTY.

He was, I think — I'm —

HELEN.

[*Laughing.*] No, no! I mean the portrait. It's higher on this side than on the other. [*Pointing.*]

POVERTY.

[*Looking.*] Fancy! [*Loud knocking at the outer door of front entrance.*] A caller, and Bullock is not here, [POVERTY *disappears for an instant and then returns.*] Mr. Maby— the old chap.

HELEN.

Is Jack with him?

POVERTY.

I'll see. [*Retires. Knocking continues.* POVERTY *is heard, calling to wait a minute. Noise of falling boards. Enters* OLD MABY, *with dust on his coat, handkerchief in hand, wiping dust of his face, followed by* POVERTY.]

OLD MABY.

Who — [*Sneezes.*] was — [*Sneezes.*] the last man who entered that door. [*Sneezes.*] I'm nearly choked. [*Turns and looks at entrance.*]

POVERTY.

The sheriff.

OLD MABY.

And the man before him?

POVERTY.

Another sheriff, I think — I'm not sure.

OLD MABY.

Are you sure it wasn't William the Conqueror. [*Laughs.*] Well, well, my lord! [*Looking about him.*] how are you?

POVERTY.

Busy. I'm straightening matters up, to go to America. [HELEN *disappears through arched entrance.*]

OLD MABY.

[*Looking about.*] Straightening matters up eh? You'll be busy then for the winter.

POVERTY.

A few hours.

OLD MABY.

[*Laughing.*] You're booked for Saturday, yes, yes. Say, say — why in the devil did you let Rushfoot get into this scrape?

POVERTY.

The duel?

OLD MABY.

You're liable to arrest, at any moment. In fact the police are stirring.

POVERTY.

Of course.— So are we.

OLD MABY.

Say, say, is Bradford badly hurt?

POVERTY.

Cheek grazed, and part of his ear gone. Only one shot.

OLD MABY.

Where is Bradford?

POVERTY.

On the way to Belgium. When we quit, they'll not have evidence enough to justify a warrant. In six months the affair will be forgotten.

OLD MABY.

Where are the folks?

POVERTY.

In the Annie repacking their luggage.

OLD MABY.

The "Annie"?

POVERTY.

Yes, the Queen Annie, the wing — the modern end. [*Pointing.*]

OLD MABY.

Modern! [*Laughing to himself.*]

POVERTY.

Built in seventeen and eighteen.

OLD MABY.

From the way they got out of Devon House,

I should think they'd need to repack. [*Laughing.*] I must see Rushfoot. By the way, you've heard about the big strike on the Extension.

POVERTY.

Yes, I'm looking for me shares.

OLD MABY.

Where is Smile and Gower now! [*Laughing.*]

POVERTY.

Fancy! [*Enters* HELEN.]

OLD MABY.

The shares closed yesterday at twenty seven pounds.

POVERTY.

[*To himself.*] I must find me shares.

HELEN.

[*Aside.*] Where is Jack? [*To* OLD MABY.] Pardon me, Mr. Maby, did anyone call after we left?

OLD MABY.

Nobody—

HELEN.

[*Aside.*] Oh dear!

OLD MABY.

Except the art chap and Miss Revere. They rode over with me. [To POVERTY.] Say, say, your driveway is in bad shape, it needs repairing.

POVERTY.

New dirt — of course.

OLD MABY.

The critic and Miss Revere jumped out to save themselves from being dumped. [*Laughs.*]

HELEN.

[*Aside.*] Jack and Effie here. I'll get my hat. [*Goes to left entrance.*]

OLD MABY.

[*To* HELEN.] Wait — do you know the ramifications of the "Annie" [*Laughs to himself.*]

HELEN.

Follow me.

OLD MABY.

[*To* POVERTY.] Say, say, Extension twenty seven pounds! [*Laughs. Exeunt* HELEN *and* OLD MABY.]

POVERTY.

Fancy' I've three thousand shares. I'm no hand at figures. [*Reflects.*] The noughts from three thousand leaves three; three times seven is twenty one — I've used the noughts and the seven up, Three times twenty is sixty and twenty one are eighty one — with the used up noughts added, make eighty one thousand, and then the pounds! That's it! eighty one thousand pounds. But I can't find me shares. [*Enter* JACK *and* EFFIE *through the arched hallway.* JACK *appears doubtful as tho where the entrance leads. Looks in.*]

JACK.

[*Without seeing* POVERTY.] This is—

EFFIE.

[*Looking.*] So it is.

POVERTY.

[*Hearing* EFFIE'S *voice.*) Come in Maloney! why not?

JACK.

[*With dignity.*] I'm here Lord Poverty.

POVERTY.

Of course — you're as good as your word.

EFFIE.

I'm out of breath.

POVERTY.

[*Rings;* EFFIE *starts,* JACK *smiles.*] It takes the wind out one to shank Poverty Hill. [*To* EFFIE.] You'll have some water.

EFFIE.

No, no thank you. [POVERTY *rings twice,*] I really don't care for any.

POVERTY.

Of course. Two bells mean "don't come Bullock."

JACK.

[*Aside.*] I wish some of our lord cracked American girls could see Poverty Castle. [*Laughs.*]

EFFIE.

[*To* POVERTY.] Where is Miss Rushfoot?

POVERTY.

This way — [*Pointing to left entrance.*] I'll show you. [*Going toward left entrance.*]

EFFIE.

Thank you.

POVERTY.

If Mr. Randolph will pardon me.

JACK.

[*Who has been looking at pictures.*] Certainly. [*Exeunt* EFFIE *and* POVERTY. *Enters* HELEN *from arched hall way.*]

HELEN.

[*Doesn't see* JACK.] Oh dear! where is he? [*Sees* JACK — *starts.*] My!

JACK.

[*Sarcastically.*] Looking for Lord Poverty no doubt.

HELEN.

No I'm not looking for Lord Poverty, but for my great big ninny John Randolph Robins Jr. [*Kisses him.*]

JACK.

[*Indifferently.*] Thank you.

HELEN.

[*Looks at* JACK.] For what, the kiss or the complement?

JACK.

I don't want you to kiss me again.

HELEN.

I will. I'll kiss you as much as I chose.

JACK.

[*Working his foot.*] I know how to suffer.

HELEN.

So do I. Horrible! [*Making faces.*] you've been smoking.

JACK.

His lordship don't smoke.

HELEN.

He smokes too— It's perfectly awful.

JACK.

What?

HELEN.

The odor of an English pipe. Jack, you're jealous.

JACK.

You're mistaken.

HELEN.

Not jealous?

JACK.

No, not jealous, but aped on.

HELEN.

[*Seriously.*] You've been wronged Jack, but not aped on.

JACK.

I've been monkied with, any way.

HELEN.

That of course, I know, but not aped on

JACK.

[*With indignation.*] Monkied with! Have I been brought back from Liverpool to have my lacerated heart anointed with vitrol?

HELEN.

Now Jack, you stop! You joined me in my exile, didn't you? and why? Because you knew I loved you and of course, anybody could see, that you loved me. We wanted to be together. To do so, you had your hoodwinking to do, I had mine — Lord Poverty had his. I was to pretend to love Lord Poverty, when Benson was about, in order that he might love Effie under cover. Lord Poverty was to make out that he loved me, in order that you and I might—

JACK.

Might what?

HELEN.

Spoon it — without being suspected. That's the English of it.

JACK.

Why didn't I get the tip?

HELEN.

[*Snappishly.*] Lord Poverty blundered, he was to tell you but he didn't. I thought you were in the scheme.

JACK.

The whole affair is enveloped, even yet in a slight London atmosphere.

HELEN.

It is!

JACK.

Why should my impudence have been discussed by your father.

HELEN.

Your impudence! what are you talking about Jack?

JACK.

About "cheek brass, and sublime confidence."

HELEN.

[*Affecting to fall in despair.*] Oh! [*Snappishly.*] Father has never talked about you!

JACK.

[*Surprised.*] No?

HELEN.

'Twas brother George. [*Snappishly.*] Mr. George Maby.

JACK.

[*Approaching* HELEN.] Helen dear!

HELEN.

[*Retreating.*] Jack Robins — you keep away from me. [*Affecting to cry.*] Take your old steamer and go to America! [*Looking sideways at him through her fingers.*] Accuse me, of trying to pull Lord Poverty's — limb.

JACK.

Helen, you know I love you. [*Approaching her again.*]

HELEN.

You don't! [*Retreating.*] You never have! [*Going to left entrance.*] And you can see, that I'm *not dying for you.* [*Exit* HELEN.]

JACK.

[*With an air of satisfaction.*] This is business! Love — real love — true love — seasoned now and then with a little misunderstanding is heaven; but constant scrapping, peppered at long intervals, with too much love is — [*Pauses.*] I imagine — [*Looking toward front entrance and taking a cigar from his pocket.*] I'll go out and take a smoke, then I'll come back and brace the old man; tell him everything, everything. [*Exit through front entrance. Enters* POVERTY.

POVERTY.

[*Reflects.*] I think so — I'm not sure. [*Enters* HELEN.]

HELEN.

Father has just finished reading his mail. Now is a good time to tell him, that the great art critic is no other than Jack Robins Jr. that he wants to marry me — that he is awfully smart — that he's madly in love with me and things like that. Don't tell Jack!

POVERTY.

Of course — things like that. [*Exi* HELEN *through front hallway. Enters* RUSHFOOT.]

RUSHFOOT.

Well Poverty, my boy! how are you, anyway? The devil take that dueling affair! Do you know, I havn't had a minute with you, alone, since the Prince's visit.

POVERTY.

How did the celebration come off?

RUSHFOOT.

I'm awfully sorry you were n't there. 'Twas great! The Prince acted like a perfect gentleman. In his speech he said that the principal of arbitration was right — that the edicts of an impartial tribunal was preferable, to the distressing judgments of the battle field, and so on and so forth. He was very nice. Then I spoke! My boy, I was in great form. Following Wales, I said that my country and his should join hands forever — but here was my most elegant outburst. "The most perfect union in all nature, transcending the union of states, or the compact of empires— a union compared with which, the espousals of heaven, or the wedlocks of earth were but robes of sands — that union was — the union of the Siamese Twins. To these, inseparable fragments of humanity, nature pointed with indexed significance to the great possibilities of a real Anglo-American combine, with one flag, bearing upon it's folds, the imperishable motto "Arbitration and Free Trade for England — forever!" My dear boy, the American ambassador, why, he just wept with joy!

POVERTY.

Fancy! You know your daughter Helen—

RUSHFOOT.

I should say so.

POVERTY.

Of course, why not? You see, she'll be marriageable soon.

RUSHFOOT.

She's old enough now.

POVERTY.

Old enough — of course — but you see, it's

quite the thing to let a girl know her fate for a year or two. She's in love.

RUSHFOOT

Well! How about you?

POVERTY.

Me? [*Looking at* RUSHFOOT.] I don't mind telling you; the maggot is at me heart too.

RUSHFOOT.

It won't do Poverty. [*To himself.*] I'm sorry.

POVERTY.

Your permission is all that's—

RUSHFOOT.

[*Sorrowfully.*] Now Courtland, I like you, you're a descendant of the old barons; I like the children of the old baron, those medieval scamps, that swore, swaggered, and swined in times of peace — yet in the hour of peril, they forged to the front, clear up to the vizor of their enimies, smote them down or fell themselves. That's right! Sure!

POVERTY.

About Helen, you see the girl has been hoodwinking—

RUSHFOOT.

[*Interrupting.*] No she hasn't, I've heard a few things. Now, how are you fixed?

POVERTY.

How am I fixed?

RUSHFOOT.

Yes.

POVERTY.

Oh! me assets — if you've any interest in knowing, I don't mind telling you, I have an estate in Scotland.

RUSHFOOT.

Does this belong to you?

POVERTY.

Poverty Castle?

RUSHFOOT.

Yes.

POVERTY.

I've only a life interest in it. I have an estate in Scotland, a few miles of dirt and rocks, and old trees, that have been groaning away for five hundred years. Then there's the stone.

RUSHFOOT.

A quarry?

POVERTY

No, the rocks of the castle. Some bridge building chaps offer to buy the stone.

RUSHFOOT.

[*Earnestly.*] Don't tear the castle down — why, sell it!

POVERTY.

Could I now?

RUSHFOOT.

Sure if you can manage to throw in a title with the rocks.

POVERTY.

A title goes with the jail.

RUSHFOOT.

Jail! I thought it was a castle?

POVERTY.

A castle — of course — to be sure; but you see, me great, great grandfather leased it as a jail, or mad house once — I think — I'm not sure; and there's me three thousand shares —

RUSHFOOT.

[*Interrupting.*] If a title goes with the castle, you can sell it to any widow in New York, among the four thousand. It don't matter, my boy, whether it's a castle, jail or lunatic asylum; provided the title gives the purchaser the right to sit even on the royal woodpile, and look into the Queen's kitchen. [HELEN *appears in front hallway walking on tiptoes. On reaching front entrance, beckons* POVERTY. *The latter makes an excuse to approach* HELEN, *just as* RUSHFOOT *finishes his last speech* HELEN *whispers to* POVERTY.]

POVERTY.

[*To* HELEN.] We havn't got to the point yet.

HELEN.

[*To* POVERTY.] Make way for Jack then, he's coming to the front like a man. [HELEN *disappears.*]

POVERTY.

[*To* RUSHFOOT.] Of course — to be sure. [*Putting his hand in his pocket, as though searching for a paper.*] Pardon me a moment, I had an inventory of me assets. Where can it be? [*Goes to left entrance.*] Just a moment. [*Exit* POVERTY.]

RUSHFOOT.

[*Shaking his head.*] No — England claims one child, she shall have only one; yet Poverty is a good fellow. [HELEN *and* JACK *appear in the hallway.* HELEN *kisses him, while he straightens up preparatory to his interview with* RUSHFOOT. *Enters* JACK.]

JACK.

[*Coughing.*] Mr. Rushfoot. [*With nervous dignity.*]

RUSHFOOT.

Why Randolph! how are you? [*Takes* JACK'S

hand. HELEN *is seen peeping around the corner of left pillar.*]

JACK.

Randolph is not my — name.

RUSHFOOT.

[*Aside.*] What impertinence! [*To* JACK *snappishly.*] Mr. Randolph, does that suit you better?

JACK.

No, no, Mr. Rushfoot, you don't understand me. My full name is, John Jack — Ran — dolph. [*Disgusted with himself.*]

RUSHFOOT.

Oh, I see! [*Laughing.*] You take no exception to Randolph.

JACK.

No sir. I trust that some day, you will do me the honor of calling me your so — your Jack — just Jack — ordinary Jack — just Randolph Jack [*Aside.*] This is tough!

RUSHFOOT.

[*Laughing and shaking his head.*] Sure! I

had a friend named Jack once, Jack— [*Reflecting.*] Robins. We were boys together. He was the wildest devil I ever knew, and they tell me, that he's got a son that's a terror.

JACK.

How did your friend Jack Robins pan out?

RUSHFOOT.

[*Deliberately.*] Oh, all right as a man, but as a boy — My heavens! Cheek! He had an effulgent front, that would make a horse shy.

JACK.

Have you ever seen his son?

RUSHFOOT.

No, nor I don't want to! [HELEN *in despair.*] But Jack, how are you, you're an art critic?

JACK.

[*Aside.*] I'll give him a sample off my effulgent front. [*To* RUSHFOOT.] Art critic, yes sir,— an art critic, that's what I pretend to be. I'm clever and ambitious.

RUSHFOOT.

That's good, that's the way to talk. [*Aside.*] Just a little gall. [*To* JACK.] Ambitious, that's right.

JACK.

Ambitious to get married,

RUSHFOOT.

Why don't you?

JACK.

With your permission, I will.

RUSHFOOT.

[*Surprised.*] My permission?

JACK.

Yes, Mr. Rushfoot, with your consent, I'll marry your lovely daughter. Helen's anxious, and I'm willing, no, no the anxiety is here! [*Pointing to himself.*]

RUSHFOOT.

[*With surpressed indignation.*] Have you been making love to my daughter, sir?

JACK.

[*Earnestly and looking* RUSHFOOT *in the face.*] I have! I'm a man of taste!

RUSHFOOT.

[*Cooling down.*] Admirable taste, but— [*Enters* POVERTY, RUSHFOOT *looks at* POVERTY *and then at* JACK. *Aside.*] Great Scott! how many more? This makes three, counting that young scamp in America, Jack Robins.

POVERTY.

I can't find me inventory.

RUSHFOOT.

Never mind, Poverty.

POVERTY.

[*Looking at* RUSHFOOT *and then at* JACK.] Am I in the way?

JACK.

Not in my way?

POVERTY.

[*To* RUSHFOOT.] Of course not. Marriage after all is only a womans question. Men bother around about it, on the day of show — that's all — I think — I'm not sure.

RUSHFOOT.

[*To* POVERTY.] Do you know, that Mr. Randolph is also in love with my daughter?

JACK.

[*To himself — surprised.*] Also in love?

POVERTY.

I don't know about the also chap, but I do know about Jack, he wants to take Helen over.

RUSHFOOT.

Take her over?

POVERTY.

Yes — marry her — why not?

RUSHFOOT.

[*Looking at* JACK, *and then at* POVERTY *aside.*] This

is mysterious! [*To* POVERTY.] Not five minutes ago, you were asking my consent —

POVERTY.

To be sure — to let Jack have her.

RUSHFOOT.

[*Aside.*] Oh, that's different! There's one third of the mystery solved.

JACK.

I didn't ask anybody to intercede in my behalf, I'm man enough to face the music myself.

RUSHFOOT.

I think you are. [*Aside.*] I'll floor him! [*To* JACK.] Assuming that you're a gentleman, and not addicted to the use of brandy, I'll discuss this question, even in the presence of his lordship. When my daughter marries, I shall give her two hundred thousand dollars. What will you give her?

JACK.

Two hundred and one thousand.

RUSHFOOT.

Are you a man of fortune?

JACK.

I'll cover your money and raise you one.

RUSHFOOT.

Who are you anyway?

JACK.

John Randolph Robins, Jr.

RUSHFOOT.

[*Looking at* JACK.] So you are, and a chip of the old block. [*Surveying him.*] So you're Jack Robin's son.

POVERTY.

Of course — the art critic.

RUSHFOOT.

[*Aside.*] Two thirds of the mystery is cleared up. Well, well, well. [*To* JACK.] You'll permit me a little breathing spell, wont you.

POVERTY.

[*To* JACK, *pleadingly.*] Of course — why not?

JACK.

A short one, yes.

RUSHFOOT.

[*Going toward left entrance.*] Is it possible? [*Looks at* JACK.] Yes, the other third vanishes, [*Exit* RUSHFOOT.]

HELEN.

[*Enters from arched entrance.*] Come on Jack

JACK.

Hurrah! [*To* POVERTY.] Come on, let's get out. Hurrah!

POVERTY.

Why not? [*Exeunt* JACK, HELEN *and* POVERTY. HELEN *and* JACK *are seen embracing.* POVERTY *congratulating them. Enters* MRS. MABY *followed by* MR. MABY.]

MR. MABY.

Her treachery was fiendish — she ought to suffer.

MRS. MABY.

She does. Read her letter.

MR. MABY.

[*Refusing letter.*] No, no! Forget her.

MRS. MABY

She has left Dorchester Oaks for good — London is to be her future home. Poor sinful Lizzie. Gone! Out of my life forever!

MR. MABY.

Come, let us wander through the labyrinths of this historical old place. [*Exeunt* MR. *and* MRS. MABY. *Enters* HELEN *and* EFFIE *through main hallway, the latter laughing half hysterically.*]

HELEN.

[*Out of breath.*] Think of Lord Poverty forgetting to tell Jack. [*Laughs.*] Oh, how he did mix us all up!

EFFIE.

You and Jack are mixed up for good now, aren't you? [*Laughing.*] Oh dear!

HELEN.

[*Sentimentally.*] Forever and forever! Father hasn't said the word yet, but it's all right. I must get a wrap, Jack made me come back and get one. He's so careful of me. [*To* EFFIE.] Why don't you get engaged it's so nice? Do please, for my sake.

EFFIE.

[*Laughing.*] For your sake?

HELEN.

[*Earnestly.*] I mean for Lord Poverty's sake. He loves you, and he's got money now. Of course, I wouldn't sacrifice you to a lord, unless he had money — of course not.

EFFIE.

You think he loves me?

HELEN.

I *know* he does! [*Tragically.*] I swear he does! [*Looking at* EFFIE *with a knowing glance.*] And I know something more than that.

EFFIE.

What, pray?

HELEN.

You love him. [*Tragically.*] I'll swear to that too.

EFFIE.

[*Seriously. Putting her arm around* HELEN.] You happy, happy, dear girl! You are an American, I will tell you all. Lord Poverty is a strange man, different from all men, in all ways. To be sure, my life has been a narrow one, but I'm not giving you my little opinion. Men and women, who have lived abroad in the world, say the same thing. He sought me, a poor girl, forced by fate to abide in a land, and among a people, that my father, my mother knew not; he has asked me to become his wife. Helen, I would, if Bruce Buckingham were here to give — his consent, for I d— I do love him. I have tried to laugh the thought out of my life, but in vain. Yes, Helen my happy girl, I love Lord Poverty. Some mysterious, undefinable influence tells me, that I shall be his wife, but not until Bruce Buckingham consents. [*Making an effort to laugh.*] So you see I shall have to wait.

HELEN.

Does Lord Poverty know you are only waiting?

EFFIE.

[*Shaking her head.*] No!

HELEN.

Here he comes. Oh, Jack will scold for keeping him waiting so long. [*Exit* HELEN. *Enters* POVERTY.[

POVERTY-

You're alone Miss Revere? You see I must call you that hereafter — of course — why not?

EFFIE.

Please don't Lord Poverty.

POVERTY.

Some day, when you're married, I might call you Maloney, when your husband was about; it would be awkward, you know.

EFFIE.

I shall never marry.

POVERTY.

You won't now, Fancy!

EFFIE.

Never!

POVERTY.

[*Looking at* EFFIE.] You will make a good spinster? [*Rings.*] Of course— why not? You've been a fine girl, Maloney — I've had me eye on you. You see, the world thinks, that any sort of feminine rubbish is good enough for a wife, that an old maid is good for nothing. They forget, that in the matrimonial market, the best stuff is often left over. It gets shop worn, why not?— but the quality is there. [*Enters* BULLOCK. *To* BULLOCK.] Bullock fetch me *old* assets.

BULLOCK.

Himmediatly, me lud. [BULLOCK *retires.*]

EFFIE.

The same hold true of bachelors, does it not?

POVERTY.

Why not?

EFFIE.

You'll marry some time, my lord.

POVERTY.

[*Looking at* EFFIE *with marked earnestness.*] If I wait until you're shop worn, will you have me? Of course— you might chance me then.

EFFIE.

[*Bashfully.*] How long are you to be in America?

POVERTY.

[*Turning his head slowly and looking at* EFFIE *in slight astonishment.*] Not till you're shop worn. You've color enough in your face to last for years — wrinkles don't come in a day. I'll come back — why not? — and watch you decay. You might have a bad spell for a year or two, of course— then you'd wear quick. You know a woman without beauty, is like a soldier without a gun. She surrenders at the word. I'll knock about alone — [*Looking at* EFFIE.] until your cheeks fade.

EFFIE.

Lord Poverty, I believe you love me.

POVERTY.

Why not? You see I've always been — [*To himself.*] mushed — mushed — that's not it — squashed — yes — that's it. I've always — [*Hesitates.*] wanted you.

EFFIE.

[*Approaches* POVERTY. *Solemnly and with eyes fixed on the floor.*] Lord Poverty, I love you. Though I love you, I can not become your wife without the consent — [*Enters* BULLOCK *carrying old steamer trunk. On the end, painted in black letters, is the name* "BRUCE BUCKINGHAM" *sticking out front beneath the cover, is a quantity of straw. As* BULLOCK *approaches the table, where he places the trunk, the straw falls on to the floor.*]

POVERTY.

You've been gone long, Bullock.

BULLOCK.

Yes me lud, Hi'ad to clear haway the rubbish. When Hi placed the trunk him the Harches Tower, Hi must 'ave left the top hup, me lud.

POVERTY.

[*Opening the trunk, and slowly wiping his hands with handkerchief.*] You left the top up, of course. The straw from the rack above has been falling on me assets.

EFFIE.

[*Aside.*] I must control my feelings. I have for months and I shall continue to. I'll laugh yes laugh. [*Struggling with her emotions. To* POVERTY.] Do you keep your valuables in the stable?

POVERTY.

No, in the tower. I've lost the only valuable asset I had. If it isn't here, it's no where. [*Opens the trunk.* EFFIE *approaches the table,* POVERTY *takes straw out and throws it on the floor.* POVERTY *looks into the trunk with an odd gaze.* EFFIE *starts.*] Here Bullock— [*Taking a* CAT *from the trunk.*] you needn't mind the other cat.

BULLOCK.

[*Who has been picking up straw from floor.*] Very well, me lud. [*Takes cat and goes to left entrance.*]

EFFIE.

[*Laughing.*] Is that your valuable asset?

POVERTY.

[*Taking* KITTENS *from the trunk.*] Bullock!

BULLOCK.

Yes, me lud. [*Turns; trys to conceal a broad smile on seeing the kittens. Approaches* POVERTY.]

POVERTY.

Be careful of the cat. [*Hands* BULLOCK *kittens.*]

BULLOCK.

Yes, me lud.

POVERTY.

It's the only asset I've got, that pays a dividend. [BULLOCK *retires with cat and kittens,*]

EFFIE.

[*Who has been taken with a fit of uncontrolable laughter.*] Oh dear! Pardon me! [*Continues to laugh. Goes to front entrance greatly embarrassed.*]

POVERTY.

[*Looking at* EFFIE.] You see the cat was not the asset I was after. [*Looks in trunk.*] What's this? [*Takes bundle of papers from trunk,*] Here are me shares. [*Examining different documents.*] I think so — I'm [*Looks at paper.*] not — yes, here they are. [*To* EFFIE.] You said you couldn't become me wife, unless some one consented.

EFFIE.

[*Who still laughs, and in evident distress. Nods.*] Yes. [*Laughs.*]

POVERTY.

[*With shares in hand, looks at* EFFIE.] Who's the chap? [*Shuts down cover of trunk.*]

EFFIE.

[*Who sees the name* — "BRUCE BUCKINGHAM" *on end of trunk, still laughing, now hysterically.* POVERTY *takes her by the hand.* EFFIE *half unconsciously staggers to the trunk, throws herself on it.*] Bruce Buckingham! [*Now weeping and laughing.*]

POVERTY.

[*To* BULLOCK, *who appears at left entrance, looking for more straw.*] Brandy, quick!

BULLOCK.

Yes me lud. [BULLOCK *retires.*]

POVERTY.

[*Leads* EFFIE *to a sofa.*] Sit down. —

why not? [*Aside.*] They tell me a shock is good for hysteria. [*Kisses her. To* EFFIE.] I'm Bruce Buckingham. An other shock (*Kisses her again.*) I consent.

EFFIE.

[*Starts.*] What?

POVERTY.

It's your medicine. [*Enters* BULLOCK *with brandy bottle and a glass.* POVERTY *pours some into a glass and offers it to* EFFIE.] It's brandy. [EFFIE *drinks.*]

EFFIE.

[*Standing up.*] Oh! [*Looks at* POVERTY.] You Bruce Buckingham?

POVERTY.

Of course — why not?

EFFIE.

[*Throws her arms around* POVERTY'S *neck.*] Then my dream is true! [*Kisses him.*]

POVERTY.

[*Kisses* EFFIE *and looks at audience.*] Why not; [*To* EFFIE.] I'll tell you all about it, when we get on the steamer.

EFFIE.

Steamer?

POVERTY.

Yes, you're going to America with us. You see, my full name, cutting off a yard at each end, is Bruce Courtland, Phellps, Buckingham, Poverty. [*Enter* HELEN *and* JACK.]

HELEN.

[*Seeing* POVERTY *with his arm supporting* EFFIE.] Oh, have you—?

EFFIE.

[*Approaches trunk and leans against it.*] Yes.

POVERTY.

[*To* HELEN.] Yes, I'm to take her over.

HELEN.

[*Clapping her hands.*] I'm so happy! [*To*

POVERTY.] She loved you all the time. [*To* EFFIE, *kissing her.*] You see, I wasn't pulling his— [*Whispers.*] for a title. [EFFIE *smiles*, HELEN *laughs.*]

JACK.

[*Shakes* POVERTY'S *hand.*] Here comes a lucky man.

HELEN.

[*Who sees her father approaching the left entrance.*] Lucky?

JACK.

Yes, to get me for a son-in-law. [*To* RUSHFOOT, *who is followed by* MR. *and* MRS. MABY.] How about that breathing spell?

RUSHFOOT.

I've had it. Every one in this Castle is your friend, and I am too. [*Shakes* JACK'S *hand.*] Look here, 'twas that brandy that did it. You had a good chance to play the goody, goody sneak, and you didn't. Jack [*In a low voice.*] let me off for a hundred thousand wont you?

JACK.

Ask Helen.

RUSHFOOT.

[*Putting his arm around* HELEN.] You will wont you?

HELEN.

[*Looks at* JACK *who shakes his head.*] Father I can't.

RUSHFOOT.

Well children, God bless you!

MRS. MABY.

[*Laughing and kissing* JACK.] I never dreamed of having a great art critic for a brother. [*Enters* OLD MABY, *talks with his son who points to* HELEN, JACK, POVERTY *and* EFFIE.]

JACK.

[*Pulling from his pocket a pair of cuffs covered with writing.*] Please accept these, as a souvenir of my first criticism.

MRS. MABY.

[*Taking cuffs laughs.*] Thank you.

OLD MABY.

[*To* JACK, *laughing.*] Say, say *you* havn't been fishing for soap? You've got enough of your own. [*To all.*] Harry rode over and brought the news "Sirao pleaded guilty, and got five years" Maxey is doing well and clapped his hands for joy, when he heard that he was to go back to Italy. [*To* MR. MABY.] The agreement you make, for his support and education, will be completed and ready for your signature, tomorrow. The papers say you are to be knighted.

ALL.

Good, good!

RUSHFOOT.

[*To* POVERTY, *who has been talking to* EFFIE. *Low music,* LIFE ON THE OCEAN WAVE.] Well Courtland my boy, you're going to marry. That's right sure! Be happy, live in peace and in America.

POVERTY.

Of course. You see, if Maloney and I have any nisunderstandings, we'll submit the thing to arbitration.

RUSHFOOT.

That's right! Let *your* motto be "Maloney and Poverty — for Maloney — forever."

POVERTY.

Of course. [*To* RUSHFOOT.] I'll sell me castle in Scotland.

RUSHFOOT.

Your jail. [*Laughing.*]

POVERTY.

Of course. Sell me jail to the four thousand New York widows, and live in America,

EFFIE.

Yes, beneath the blue skies.

POVERTY.

Of course — why not?

[THE END.]

Printed by G. JACOB, MANNHEIM (Germany).

www.ingramcontent.com/pod-product-compliance
Lightning Source LLC
Chambersburg PA
CBHW031944230426
43672CB00010B/2049